"Read and pray your way though this Advent book, and your Christmas may be very different from previous ones. Or rather, you may be a very different person this Christmas, which is rather more important. Of course, it's not all about you; it's all about Jesus Christ. But if you are *in* Christ, then actually it is all about you too. Tim Chester fills out the wonderful words of Paul in Philippians with delightfully written, short reflections, full of fresh images and comparisons, and in a style that is very easy to read, though these truths are less easy to live. You'll feed on some very rich biblical theology, bite-sized but deeply nourishing."

Chris Wright,
International Ministries Director, Langham Partnership

"The Christmas season can often be marked by a time of increase: a frenzied pace, material splurges, and even personal grumbling. What often gets drowned out is a quiet and refreshing contemplation of timeless truth. In this short but accessible series of Advent devotions, Tim Chester invites us to go from muttering to marvelling this Christmas by considering the most compelling man who ever lived: Jesus Christ."

Erik Raymond,
Senior Pastor, Emmaus Bible Church, Omaha,
and The Gospel Coalition blogger

"Tim Chester's writing is clear and fresh, and allows the light of God's word to shine brightly. I am looking forward to using Tim's book in Advent and I hope many will too. Advent focuses on true gifts which we neglect at our peril; there is accountability, there is a God who cares, there is a universe in which the kingdom of God has come and will come. Don't let Advent be taken over by Christmas; use Tim's book to discover more of the one true gift."

The Right Reverend Keith Sinclair,
Bishop of Birkenhead

Tim Chester

The One True Gift

Daily Readings for Advent to Encourage and Inspire

The One True Gift
© Tim Chester/The Good Book Company, 2017.

Published by
The Good Book Company
Tel (UK): 0333 123 0880
International: +44 (0) 208 942 0880
Email: info@thegoodbook.co.uk

Websites:
UK: www.thegoodbook.co.uk
North America: www.thegoodbook.com
Australia: www.thegoodbook.com.au
New Zealand: www.thegoodbook.co.nz

ISBN: 9781784982225 | Printed in the UK

Design by André Parker

Contents

Introduction
The One True Gift

Christmas is supposed to be a time of "peace on earth and goodwill to all men".

And we all fondly imagine our family gathered round a roaring fire. The children giggle as they play their board game. Your teenager is making a cup of tea for her grandmother. Your elderly neighbour is sitting happily in his new hand-knitted jumper. Then someone asks Grandad for an old story. You look across at your spouse and smile a smile of contented satisfaction. Peace and goodwill.

But the reality of Christmas can be very different! The children are fighting over the television remote. Your teenager only left her room after dire threats and is now sulking in the corner underneath her headphones. Your elderly neighbour isn't there because he and Grandad refuse to be in the same room together. And you and your spouse are still not talking after last night's argument. There's little goodwill around and your only moment of peace comes when you take the dog for a walk.

Or perhaps these are problems that you'd love to have. But your Christmas will be tinged with grief and loneliness, not peace and goodwill, as you remember the relationships you've lost.

All too often Christmas descends into grumbling or arguing. You mutter under your breath about the shameless commercialisation, the competing crowds of shoppers, the dark, cold evenings. Your wife grumbles about the extra chores or your husband grumbles about visiting his in-laws. And you can't get the children to do anything without an argument.

And then in Philippians 2 v 14 Paul says:

> *Do everything without grumbling or arguing.*

Can you imagine a grumble-free Christmas? An argument-free zone? Not me.

But Paul doesn't merely taunt us with an unattainable ideal. He wraps it up in a wonderful description of the one true Christmas gift—the Lord Jesus Christ. The one true gift radically alters our perspective on our grumbles and arguments. So over the next 24 days, we'll peel back the layers on this passage from Philippians, and enjoy afresh God's gift to us at Christmas.

Philippians 2 v 6-11 was probably an early Christian hymn. Whether Paul himself wrote it or whether he's quoting lyrics familiar to his readers is unclear. Maybe he quotes an existing hymn, but adds his own tweaks for extra emphasis. We can't be sure. What matters is that Paul and the Holy Spirit thought these were the words the Philippians needed to hear. And these are still words we need to hear.

Philippians 2 invites us to step into the Christmas story in a way that radically reshapes our attitudes.

You may not be able to change the behaviour of your family. There may still be arguments fizzing around this Christmas. But *you* can encounter Christ afresh this Christmas in a way that will make you a bearer of peace and goodwill.

Born to set an example

"Therefore if you have any encouragement from being united with Christ, if any comfort from his love, if any common sharing in the Spirit, if any tenderness and compassion, then make my joy complete by being like-minded, having the same love, being one in spirit and of one mind. Do nothing out of selfish ambition or vain conceit. Rather, in humility value others above yourselves, not looking to your own interests but each of you to the interests of the others. In your relationships with one another, have the same mindset as Christ Jesus."

Philippians 2 v 1-5

Everyone loves Jesus.

Church attendance is falling. It's common to hear people say they have no time for organised religion. Plenty of people despise Christianity. But still they like the person at its heart.

Jesus is respected as a good man. After all, he was concerned for the poor and associated with outcasts. He told us to love our enemies and turn the other cheek—which sounds good, even if most of us don't do it very much.

In reality most people have a Christmas-card version of Jesus. It's all rather sanitised and safe. Christmas-card Jesus wears a permanent smile, and only ever says nice things that make us feel good about ourselves.

But the real Jesus that we meet in the Gospels is not quite so tame. For one thing, he could be rude. He said it straight. Much of what he said—about his uniqueness, about sexuality, about judgment—cuts right across the grain of our culture.

And yet… Jesus remains a compelling figure. When he was rude, it was to confront the injustice of his day. When he said it straight, it was to warn us in love.

In Jesus we see the epitome of love and goodness. He is the perfect man. He is perfect in his mercy, perfect in his justice, perfect in his speech, perfect in his attitudes, perfect in his anger, perfect in his love. His life is compelling and attractive.

∽

Christians are people who want to be like Jesus. That's what Paul says here in verse 5:

> *In your relationships with one another, have the same mindset as Christ Jesus.*

Jesus was born to set an example. There is so much more he came to do. Indeed, if he had just come to set an example, then the message of Jesus would be bad news. For his example would only condemn us. None of us could live up to his standards. So there is much more to say about Jesus.

But there isn't less to say: he *is* our example.

Paul picks out one idea in particular here in Philippians 2 (or a cluster of related ideas): "Value others above yourselves, not looking to your own interests but each of you to the interests of the others" (v 3-4). He's writing to a church and describing the life that should characterise a church community. But the same principles apply in your family, your workplace or your neighbourhood. We need to put others first. Think about how Jesus did these things.

- **"Do nothing out of selfish ambition or vain conceit." (v 3)** Jesus left the glory of heaven to share our pain. He came to a context where no one recognised his status as the Son of God. Jesus wasn't a social climber! He wasn't clambering up the greasy pole. He wasn't dreaming of his next big promotion. He didn't have his eye on a bigger house. His trajectory was in the opposite direction. His "ambition" drove him *down* to earth.

- **"In humility value others above yourselves." (v 3)** The attitude of Jesus was epitomised in the moment when a group of mothers brought their children to Jesus. His disciples tried to send them away. As far as they were concerned, Jesus was far too important to hang out with little children. But that's not how Jesus saw it. "He was indignant" when he saw what was happening (Mark 10 v 14). He was happy to spend time with children—those people that his culture thought had little value.

- **"Not looking to your own interests but each of you to the interests of the others." (v 4)** This is why Jesus was born—because he put our interests before his own. And this is why Jesus was crucified. He was willing to bear the judgment we deserve so that we might be acquitted. Our interests before his interests. Putting others first.

~૭

You may not have to die for your family or colleagues today. At least, not literally. But there may be moments when you need to die to self. Your status and interests are quietly executed as you put others first.

Now why would you do that? Paul gives us some reasons in verse 1: the encouragement of being united with Christ; the comfort of his love; our common sharing in the Spirit; and the tenderness and compassion the Lord Jesus gives.

But the most surprising reason is in verse 2: the prospect of making our "joy complete". What gives Paul joy? It's *shared* joy. That's the goal of his ministry (1 v 25). In a strange upside-down sort of way, putting others first leads to joy. It's the joy of being like Jesus. His life is so attractive and so compelling that we're glad when we sense that in our small way we're becoming like him—and that others are too.

One day I was feeling gloomy—got-up-on-the-wrong-side-of-the-bed gloomy. And then my friend told me how God had been at work in his life, how he had overcome temptation, how my words had helped (something I'd forgotten ever saying). It turned my mood upside down—or rather, the right way up. You only get that—complete joy, shared joy—when you're investing in the lives of other people. When you're looking to *their* interests, and not your own.

Meditate

O little one sweet, O little one mild,
In thee love's beauties are all distilled.
Then light in us thy love's bright flame,
That we may give thee back the same,
O little one sweet, O little one mild.

(Traditional German carol)

~∂

Prayer

Father God,
may I, at least a little,
follow my Lord and Deliverer
as a token of my gratitude.
Lord Jesus,
I am nothing and can do nothing.
All I have is through you,
out of the grace of the Father.
I will keep nothing for myself
but with joy will put all I possess
at the service of my brethren.
May I be obedient in death,
even in the death of the cross;
that is, may I accept
all sufferings and disgrace.
Amen.

(Adapted from a prayer of German Reformer
Martin Bucer, 1491-1551)

Born to unite us to him

2

*"Have this mind among yourselves, which is yours
in Christ Jesus."*
Philippians 2 v 5 (ESV)

So how have you got on since you read the last chapter? Have you been putting others first? Have you been valuing others above yourself?

I'm sure you've had many good moments when you've been humble, generous and sacrificial. But our proud, selfish selves have a habit of gate-crashing the party. We set out with good intentions, but life never quite works out the way we intend. *We* never work out the way we intend.

My wife always makes the table look wonderful for our Christmas meal. The white tablecloth makes its annual appearance. Every place is set with the nearest thing to matching cutlery and glassware we can manage. The centre is decorated. Candles are lit. But by the end of the meal everything is in total disarray. The children have played with the candle wax. There are gravy stains all over the tablecloth. The once beautifully folded napkins are all in a crumpled heap.

That's how every day feels to me. Everything is beautiful and clean in the morning. I wake to fresh mercies from God. But all too quickly there are stains and crumples. On a meal table this mess is a sign that everyone had a good time. But that's not true of the mess in my life.

∾

The example of Jesus attracts us and inspires us. But, as we saw yesterday, on its own it also taunts and accuses us. Who can measure up? Compared to Jesus, we are stained and crumpled.

But Jesus is not just our example. Verse 5 says, "Have this mind among yourselves, which is yours in Christ Jesus" (ESV). Fundamental to Paul's point is this reality: *we are in Christ Jesus.*

Jesus was born so we could be "in him". He came to unite our humanity to his divinity—our humanness to his "God-ness". He came to be one with us so we could be one with him. We describe followers of Jesus as "Christians". But the Bible only uses that term three times (Acts 11 v 26; 26 v 28; 1 Peter 4 v 16). Much more often it describes believers as those who are *"in Christ"*. When you turn from sin and entrust yourself to Jesus, you become "in Christ".

But what does it mean to be in Christ? Think what it means to be *in a car*. If you're *in a car*, then what happens to the car happens to you. If the car starts moving, then you start moving. If it goes round a corner, then you go round the corner.

It's the same with Christ. If you're in Christ, then what happens to Christ happens to you. He bore the judgment of God, and that judgment is borne for you. He rose again, and you rise with him to eternal life.

∾

Later on in Philippians, Paul highlights one of the benefits of being "in Christ":

> *What is more, I consider everything a loss because of the surpassing worth of knowing Christ Jesus my Lord, for whose sake I have lost all things. I consider them garbage, that I may gain Christ and be found in him, not having a righteousness of my own that comes from the law, but that which is through faith in Christ—the righteousness that comes from God on the basis of faith.* (Philippians 3 v 8-9)

Did you spot the "in him" in the middle of this quote? Paul says that everything is rubbish compared with being "found in him". Why? Because, by being in Christ, Paul shares the righteousness of Christ. "Righteousness" means being *right with God*. Jesus is right with God, and if we are in Jesus, then we are right with God. And nothing matters more than that.

So being good enough for God is not something we achieve. Instead it "comes from God on the basis of faith"—it's by trusting in Jesus that we're made right with God.

Which brings me backed to my stained and crumpled life. It's as if God whips off the tablecloth of my life and gives it to Jesus to deal with. And then he throws over my life the beautiful, pristine, whiter-than-white tablecloth of Jesus. The Bible doesn't use the image of a tablecloth. But it does use the image of clothing. Galatians 3 v 27 says, "All of you who were baptised into Christ have clothed yourselves with Christ".

∽

Sometimes people have feared that this free gift of righteousness will make Christians careless about sin because any "spillages" get covered up by Christ. But that's not how it works. Which are you careful to keep clean? A clean tablecloth or a dirty tablecloth? A clean dress or a dirty dress? "Clothe yourselves with the Lord Jesus Christ, and do not think about how to gratify the desires of the flesh" (Romans 13 v 14). You have been forgiven by God. You have been united to Christ. Let that truth shape how you live today.

Meditate

He deigns in flesh to appear,
Widest extremes to join;
To bring our vileness near,
And make us all divine:
And we the life of God shall know,
For God is manifest below.

Made perfect by his love,
And sanctified by grace,
We shall from earth remove,
And see his glorious face:
Then shall his love be fully showed,
And man shall then be lost in God.

(From "Let earth and heaven combine" by Charles Wesley, 1707-1788)

∽

Prayer

O holy Child of Bethlehem, descend to us, we pray.
Cast out our sin and enter in, be born in us today.
We hear the Christmas angels the great glad tidings tell.
O come to us, abide with us, our Lord Immanuel.
(From "O little town of Bethlehem" by Phillip Brooks, 1835-1893)

Born to reshape our lives

"Have this mind among yourselves, which is yours in Christ Jesus."
Philippians 2 v 5 (ESV)

I once attended a citizenship ceremony at our local town hall. Some friends were becoming British citizens. Together with a handful of other people, they were reminded of their new privileges and responsibilities, and then they swore allegiance to the queen. Through that act their status changed. They went from being "foreigners" to being "citizens".

Or think of a wedding. The act of getting married radically changes your identity. You go from being single to being married. And as a result your behaviour changes (or at least it should). You start to act like a married person—you begin to consider your spouse as you make both small plans and big decisions.

In a similar way, putting your faith in Christ radically changes your identity. You become a citizen of heaven. That's how Paul describes Christians later in Philippians. "Our citizenship," he says in 3 v 20, "is in heaven".

As a result, our behaviour changes. We start to act in line with our new identity. We start to live as citizens of heaven—as those who are part of the bride of Christ.

~

That's what Paul means by verse 5: "Have this mind among yourselves, which is yours in Christ Jesus". He's not simply saying that we should follow Christ's example. He's saying that we should behave as those who are now in Christ Jesus. We need to start living in a way that is consistent with our new identity in Christ.

It's not that we must behave in a certain way to earn our new identity. That's not how marriage works. I don't behave like a married man so I can gradually become more and more married. My wedding makes me a 100% married man. But then I need to start acting in a way that's consistent with that new identity. That change of behaviour may be gradual—it takes time to think and act in a new way. But my change of identity is immediate. Putting your faith in Christ places you completely in Christ—100%.

And that change of status is a gift. You don't achieve it. You simply receive it by faith. But your new status changes everything.

~

In the last chapter we compared being in Christ to being in a car. Where the car goes, you go. Let's change the image slightly and think of it as being on a roller coaster. The gospel is the invitation to get on board, to put yourself in Christ.

And being in Christ turns our lives into something of a roller-coaster ride.

For where Christ goes, we go too. And look at the route he takes in Philippians 2. He starts off equal with God (v 6). Then he becomes a servant (v 7). At Christmas he's made human (v 7). Finally he humbles himself to death (v 8). Just like a roller coaster, it's down, down, down. And then it's up, up, up. God exalts him (v 9). Every knee bows before him (v 10). He ends up at "the highest place" (v 9). This is the route we're going to be following in the coming chapters. This is Paul's version of the Christmas story.

Here's the point. If you're in Christ, then where Christ goes, you go too. And sometimes that means down, down, down—being a servant, being humble, dying to self. Sometimes that means washing up for the umpteenth time. Sometimes that means opening your home to that awkward character. Sometimes that means staying late to stack chairs after yet another seasonal church event.

But the ultimate destination is always up, up, up. If you're at the back of a roller coaster, you may be at the bottom of the curve, but you can see where the front is and you can see where you're going. Jesus has already been exalted, vindicated and glorified in heaven. One day he'll be exalted, vindicated and glorified on earth. And Christ will share that glory with those who are *in him*.

The more you grasp the wonder of that, the less being number one at your family Christmas will matter. So what if the turkey is overcooked and dry? So what if you're forced to watch *Frozen* (again)? So what if everyone takes you for granted? Don't begrudge it. You're in a roller coaster that is heading to the top.

Meditate

And our eyes at last shall see him,
Through his own redeeming love.
For that Child so dear and gentle,
Is our Lord in heaven above.
And he leads his children on
To the place where he is gone.

(From "Once in royal David's city" by Cecil Frances Alexander, 1818-1895)

~ ୭

Prayer

Gracious Father, we thank you that
Christ has been imparted to us
with all his benefits,
that all his things are made ours,
that we are made members of him,
indeed one with him.
May we live remembering that
his righteousness overwhelms our sins;
his salvation wipes out our condemnation;
with his worthiness he intercedes
that our unworthiness
may not come before your sight.
May we not separate Christ from ourselves
or ourselves from him.
Rather may we hold fast
bravely with both hands
to that fellowship
by which he has bound himself to us. Amen.

(Adapted from John Calvin, 1509-1564)

Born to create a united people

"Have this mind among yourselves, which is yours in Christ Jesus."
Philippians 2 v 5 (ESV)

I s your church "they" or "we"?

Here's what I mean. Which of the following would you say?

"The church is great. Their morning services are uplifting and their provision for the children is good, although they could do more evangelism."

"The church is great. Our morning services are uplifting and our provision for the children is good, although we could do more evangelism."

"They" or "we"? Do you view the church as other than you—as a meeting you attend or a team of clergy? Or do you view the church as you together with your brothers and sisters? Do you attend or do you belong? Do you have a sense of responsibility and ownership for what happens?

Paul is not writing to individual Christians. He's writing to a church as a church. Every time he writes "you" it's you plural. In the American south they might have written "y'all", and in parts of Ireland, Scotland and Australia they would have said "yous". Paul is not just telling me as an individual how to behave. He's telling *us* as a church how to behave. *I'm* not just united with Christ (v 1). *We're* united together with Christ as one body.

There is much we can learn in these verses about how we should live as individuals in our families and in our workplaces. But we mustn't lose sight of Paul's focus: the local church. Being connected to Christ means being connected with other Christians. To think "Christ" is to think "we".

In the last chapter we saw that becoming a Christian involves a radical change of identity. Now we discover that the new identity is a *communal* identity. *I* need to think "*we*".

∽

When a man gets married, his identity changes. And he needs to start acting in line with that new identity. He can no longer do as he pleases with his time and money.

It's Friday afternoon and he gets a text from a friend. Does he want to come over to watch the match tomorrow? When he was single, he could make up his mind for himself. But he's not single anymore. His status changed radically on his wedding day. Now he's a married man. And that means he needs to consider his wife. What was she planning to do? Is she invited too? Would she want to go? In fact, it would probably be a good idea to make a phone call and consult her. Our young man's behaviour needs to catch up with his change of identity.

That's what Paul is saying in verse 5: "Have this mind among yourselves, which is yours in Christ Jesus" (ESV). In other words, think about one another as those who are united in Christ Jesus— think "we".

What does it mean to think "we"? There are lots of answers to that question. But Paul has some suggestions in verses 2-4. Notice how radically other-centred they are:

- "being like-minded"

- "having the same love"

- "being one in spirit and of one mind"

- "doing nothing out of selfish ambition or vain conceit"

- "in humility valuing others above yourselves"

- "not looking to your own interests but each of you to the interests of the others"

Christmas is often a busy time for local churches. There are extra meetings, carol services, outreach to the needy. What would it mean if you thought of all these activities as things "we" were doing? What would it mean for you to have a sense of ownership and responsibility for these events?

But don't just think about events. Think people. Christmas can be a difficult time for those who live alone or who've been bereaved or who are away from home. Are there people like that in your church? What difference would it make for you to think of them as "we"?

∽

Above all, our model is Jesus. Jesus left the glory of heaven, became a servant, was made human, became obedient to death. Why? Because he didn't think "they"—he thought "we". This is how Hebrews 2 v 11-15 explains what happened at the first Christmas:

*Both the one who makes people holy and those who are made
holy are of the same family. So Jesus is not ashamed to call them
brothers and sisters … Since the children have flesh and blood,
he too shared in their humanity so that by his death he might
break the power of him who holds the power of death—that is,
the devil—and free those who all their lives were held in slavery
by their fear of death.*

Christ has called you his brother or sister. He's called your church
his brothers and sisters. Now you can do the same.

Meditate

It came upon the midnight clear,
That glorious song of old,
From angels bending near the earth,
To touch their harps of gold:
"Peace on the earth, goodwill to men,
From heaven's all-gracious King."
The world in solemn stillness lay,
To hear the angels sing.

Yet with the woes of sin and strife
The world has suffered long;
Beneath the angel-strain have rolled
Two thousand years of wrong;
And man, at war with man, hears not
The love-song which they bring:
O hush the noise, ye men of strife,
And hear the angels sing.

(From "It came upon the midnight clear" by Edmund Sears, 1810-1876)

Prayer

O God the Father of our Lord Jesus Christ,
our only Saviour, the Prince of Peace:
Give us grace seriously to lay to heart
the great dangers we are in by our unhappy divisions;
take away all hatred and prejudice,
and whatever else may hinder us
from godly union and concord;
that, as there is but one Body and one Spirit,
one hope of our calling, one Lord, one Faith, one Baptism,
one God and Father of us all,
so we may be all of one heart and of one soul,
united in one holy bond
of truth and peace, of faith and charity,
and may with one mind and one mouth glorify thee;
through Jesus Christ our Lord. Amen.

(From the Book of Common Prayer)

Born to be God in a manger

"Who, being in very nature God…"
Philippians 2 v 6

When Joseph looked in the manger, what did he see? A baby—probably still slightly bloodied. Perhaps Joseph licked a piece of cloth and gently wiped the blood off.

What else did he see? A boy named Jesus.

But perhaps he also saw Immanuel, God with us. That's how the angel had described the child to Joseph: "All this took place to fulfil what the Lord had said through the prophet: 'The virgin will conceive and give birth to a son, and they will call him Immanuel' (which means 'God with us')" (Matthew 1 v 22-23).

Did Joseph really look at the baby and see his God?

∾

Verse 6 says literally that Christ Jesus was "in the form of God". That might sound as if Jesus only *appeared* to be godlike—as if he wore a "God costume". But Paul is saying much more than this.

No one can see God. But Jesus is the form of God—he is God taking shape among us. As John 1 v 18 says:

> *No one has ever seen God, but the one and only Son, who is himself God and is in the closest relationship with the Father, has made him known.*

What does God look like? What form does he take when he appears to our senses? The answer is Jesus.

Christ Jesus "was in the form of God" (Philippians 2 v 6, ESV). The word "form" here means the way the true essence of something appears to the senses. Except, of course, that God doesn't appear to our senses because he's invisible. God doesn't have a form in the way physical things do. So Paul is saying Christ has shared the majesty and glory of God. In John 17 v 5 Jesus talks about "the glory I had with [the Father] before the world began". And Hebrews 1 v 3 says, "The Son is the radiance of God's glory and the exact representation of his being". Christ completely corresponds to the being of God. So "form" doesn't mean a mask or costume. Quite the opposite. Christ's "form" displays God's *true essence*. Jesus shares the true essence of God. He is truly God.

In the New Testament, the word "form" only appears here and in the next verse. In verse 7 Jesus is in "the form of a servant", and it's clear that it doesn't mean Jesus was a pretend servant. His servanthood was real—so real that it involved him becoming human. It's the same with Jesus being in the "form of God" (v 6, ESV). He wasn't pretending to be God. He really was God. "If the form of a slave is the being of a slave," said the early church father Theodoret, "then the form of God is God." I think this is why Paul uses the word "form" in verse 6. He wants to us to spot the extraordinary movement: the One who is in the form of God takes on the form of a servant.

What does this mean as we approach Christmas? It means that the One lying in the manger was nothing less than human, and nothing less than God: God in a manger, who came to save us. After all, as Joseph looked at the child, he knew all too well that this child had not been conceived in the normal way. "What is conceived in her," the angel told Joseph, "is from the Holy Spirit" (Matthew 1 v 20).

∽

"All this took place to fulfil what the Lord had said through the prophet," said the angel to Joseph (Matthew 1 v 22). He was referring to the prophet Isaiah. Back in Isaiah's day, Judah was being invaded but King Ahaz refused to accept Isaiah's invitation to trust the LORD. Instead, Ahaz formed an alliance with Assyria. Rather predictably, it proved to be a deadly alliance; Assyria quickly turned from defender to aggressor. So Isaiah told King Ahaz, "Therefore the Lord himself will give you a sign: the virgin will conceive and give birth to a son, and will call him Immanuel" (Isaiah 7 v 14). In other words, God didn't need the family dynasty of Ahaz to fulfil his purposes. God could bring the promised Saviour-King from a virgin.

Isaiah then imagines the Assyrian army like a bird of prey, hovering over God's people. He says, "Its outspread wings will cover the breadth of your land, Immanuel!" (Isaiah 8 v 8) What does Immanuel—God-with-us—mean? Here it means God is with us in our danger and suffering. The One being in very nature God has come to share our pain. He's come to share *your* pain. God doesn't look at you from the sidelines. He's not detached or uninterested. Jesus is Immanuel. God is with us in love.

Then Isaiah adds, "Raise the war cry, you nations, and be shattered! ... Propose your plan, but it will not stand, for God is with us" (Isaiah 8 v 9-10). It's literally, "It will not stand, for Immanuel". It's almost as if Immanuel is positioned as a great roadblock into which the deadly plans of our enemies will crash. What does Immanuel mean? It means God is with us to save. God has come in the person of his Son to deliver us from our enemies.

Whatever the challenges or struggles you face this Christmas, you can know that God is with you and God is for you. The evidence is in the manger. Jesus is the great demonstration of God's commitment to us. He is Immanuel: God with us in our suffering.

Meditate
Lo, within a manger lies
He who built the starry skies;
He who, throned in height sublime,
Sits among the cherubim.
(From "See, amid the winter's snow" by Edward Caswall, 1814-1878)

∽

Prayer
O, thou precious Lord Jesus Christ,
we do adore thee with all our hearts.
Thou art Lord of all.
We bless thee for becoming man
that thou mightest be our next of kin, and being next of kin
we bless thee for taking us into marriage union with thyself
and for redeeming us and our inheritance
from the captivity into which we were sold.
Thou hast paid thy life for thy people;
thou hast ransomed thy folk with thy heart's blood.
Be thou, therefore, for ever beloved and adored. Amen.
(Charles Spurgeon, Baptist preacher, 1834-1892)

Born in submission to the Father

"Who ... did not consider equality with God something to be used to his own advantage."
Philippians 2 v 6

Jesus is not God with hand-me-down divinity. He doesn't get his divinity second-hand; instead, he shares the essence of God. He and the Father are equally divine because they share the same divine essence—two persons (three including the Holy Spirit) sharing one being. It's hard for us to get our heads round. The key thing is that Jesus is truly divine. He's not a lesser God. He is God just as the Father is God.

Yet you wouldn't think so to look in the manger. What you see in the manger is a fragile baby, totally dependent on his parents. Wait long enough—and it won't be long—and you'll see Mary dabbing away some sick or changing the first-century equivalent of a diaper.

This is the miracle of Christmas. True God became true man.

∾

What's the secret behind this miracle? It's this: Christ Jesus "did not consider equality with God something to be used to his own advantage". Jesus left the glories of heaven for us. In heaven he was worshipped by angels; on earth he was rejected by humanity. In heaven he was at home in God's glory; on earth he lay in a borrowed manger and grew up with no place to lay his head. In heaven he was surrounded by angelic armies; on earth he was threatened and finally murdered.

∾

Let's consider two amazing wonders. First, Jesus used equality with God to *our* advantage—not his own.

It's not that Jesus stopped being divine. But he didn't use his divinity for his own advantage. He didn't use it as a get-out-of-jail card to avoid the realities of the human condition. Instead, Jesus used his divinity to *our* advantage. It's not just that he refused to let his divinity get in the way of saving us. He actually used his divinity to save us. He had to. For only God could save.

This is how the 11th-century theologian Anselm put it. Sin, argued Anselm, is "not rendering to God what is his due", and the due we should give to God is our complete obedience. But we've failed to obey God, leaving us with a debt that demands satisfaction.

The problem is that there's nothing we can do to repay the debt. Anything we might offer God is part of the life of obedience we already owe him. There's no way for us to catch up with the repayments.

We owe God everything. The whole world belongs to him. So what could we give? The only thing greater than the world is God himself. So only God can make satisfaction. This creates an apparent dilemma: it's humanity who must repay the debt, but only God who has the resources to pay it.

God's radical solution is Jesus: the God-man. "None but God can make satisfaction for sin and none but man ought to make it," wrote Anselm. So "it is necessary for the God-man to make it".

~

Second wonder. Jesus combined equality with God and submission to God. Listen to a sample of the words of Jesus in John's Gospel:

> *Very truly I tell you, the Son can do nothing by himself; he can do only what he sees his Father doing, because whatever the Father does the Son also does.* (John 5 v 19)

> *By myself I can do nothing; I judge only as I hear, and my judgment is just, for I seek not to please myself but him who sent me.* (John 5 v 30)

> *For I have come down from heaven not to do my will but to do the will of him who sent me.* (John 6 v 38)

> *For I did not speak on my own, but the Father who sent me commanded me to say all that I have spoken … Whatever I say is just what the Father has told me to say.* (John 12 v 49-50)

> *The Father is greater than I … I love the Father and do exactly what my Father has commanded me.* (John 14 v 28, 31)

> *I have kept my Father's commands and remain in his love.*
> (John 15 v 10)

Jesus is equal with God and yet at the same time the Father is greater than Jesus. How do we make sense of this?

It's simple: Jesus and the Father are equal in *being*—they are both equally God, for they share one divine essence. But Jesus chooses to submit to the Father's will. He doesn't do this under compulsion. It's not that the Father in some way forces Jesus to submit. Jesus does it out of love. In love he freely submits to the Father's plan.

And what is that plan? What is the Father's will? It's us. It's you. Jesus said:

> *This is the will of him who sent me, that I shall lose none of all those he has given me, but raise them up at the last day.*
>
> (John 6 v 39)

Perhaps this Christmas you feel your hold on faith is weak and faltering. That may be so. But Christ's hold on you is firm and sure. He left the glory of heaven to rescue the people the Father had given him. And he will not lose any. He will not lose you—not if you've been given to him by his Father.

Apparently two-thirds of people receive a Christmas gift they do not like. These unwanted presents end up being returned to the store, hidden in the back of the cupboard, or just thrown away. But the Father has given Christ a gift that he will never let go of—you and me.

Meditate

O little one sweet, O little one mild,
Thy Father's purpose thou hast fulfilled.
Thou cam'st from heav'n to mortal ken,
Equal to be with us poor men,
O little one sweet, O little one mild.

(Traditional German carol)

∽

Prayer

O Lord, thou greatest and most true light,
whence this light of the day and of the sun does spring!
O Light, which does lighten every man,
that comes into this world!
O thou wisdom of the eternal Father of mercies,
enlighten my mind,
that I may only see those things that please thee
and may be blinded to all other things.
Grant that I may walk in thy ways,
and that nothing else may be light
and pleasant unto me.
Amen.

(John Bradford, English Reformer and martyr, 1510-1555)

Born in divine love

*"Who ... did not consider equality with God something
to be used to his own advantage."*
Philippians 2 v 6

A friend noticed a suspicious-looking young man in the street.
He looked dangerous and threatening, so my friend was
wary. And then, perhaps because he was distracted, he fell and hit
his head. In a busy street only one person came to his aid: the
very man he had been afraid of! Sometimes our preconceptions get
turned upside down.

∽

The prophet Isaiah once launched a full-on attempt to overturn the
preconceptions of his hearers. He invited them to compare their
idols to the living God. He mocked those who had created an idol
from a piece of wood and then thought the figure they had created
could save them (Isaiah 44). Faced with a choice between the living
God and a lump of wood, it's obvious which you're going to choose.

The problem is the choice doesn't normally come in this form. But sometimes today we're faced with two people both claiming their god is the true God or their cause is the true cause. Who are we to believe?

So to prove his credentials, in Isaiah 45 God predicts the future. His people will go into exile in Babylonian and then they'll be delivered by the Persian king Cyrus. He even name-checks Cyrus. Here's the proof that Isaiah's God is the true God for only he can foretell the future.

> *Who foretold this long ago,*
>   *who declared it from the distant past?*
> *Was it not I, the LORD?*
>   *And there is no God apart from me,*
> *a righteous God and a Saviour;*
>   *there is none but me.*   (Isaiah 45 v 21)

God then turns this truth into an appeal. Because he alone is the true God, he alone can truly save:

> *Turn to me and be saved,*
>   *all you ends of the earth;*
>   *for I am God, and there is no other.*
> *By myself I have sworn,*
>   *my mouth has uttered in all integrity*
>   *a word that will not be revoked:*
> *before me every knee will bow;*
>   *by me every tongue will swear.*   (Isaiah 45 v 22-23)

If this sounds familiar, it's because Paul is alluding to this in Philippians 2 v 10-11. "Before me every knee will bow," says God in Isaiah. "At the name of Jesus every knee should bow," says Paul in Philippians. "By me every tongue will swear," says God in Isaiah. "And every tongue [will] acknowledge that Jesus Christ is Lord," says Paul in Philippians.

~

But there are two radical twists to what Paul is saying.

First, Paul is talking about a man: Jesus. Paul is claiming that Jesus is the true God. Not only that, but Paul uses an Old Testament passage that says, "There is no God apart from me" to say that Jesus is God.

At first sight Isaiah 45 looks as if it might prove that Jesus is *not* God. After all, the LORD in Isaiah couldn't be clearer: "I am God, and there is no other". And now another has appeared.

Or another possibility is that Isaiah was wrong and there are two Gods: the LORD and Jesus. But Isaiah was speaking on God's behalf. Besides which, if Paul thought Isaiah was wrong, then he wouldn't have quoted him to declare the victory of Jesus.

No, we are left with this conclusion: the baby in the manger is none other than the LORD, the covenant God of Israel, the Creator, the one, true God.

~

But what evidence does Paul give for the divinity of Jesus? Here's where we get our second even more amazing twist. What has Paul told us about Christ Jesus? That he "did not consider equality with God something to be used to his own advantage". The evidence that Jesus is God is that he acted in an un-godlike way. Or rather, Jesus acted in a way that we would never have expected the living God to act.

God in the person of Jesus Christ is acknowledged as God not because he has done godlike things in terms of human notions of God. It's not because he has acted in power or revealed himself in a blaze of glory. Jesus is acknowledged as God because he has humbled himself, and submitted to the cruel and shameful death of crucifixion.

The cross alone reveals the radical, gracious freedom of God. God alone is so free that he can discount "equality with God" and offer himself in love for his people. God alone is so gracious that he freely chooses to be God-forsaken to reconcile himself with those who have rejected him. Nothing demonstrates the "God-ness" of God so much as the godlessness of the cross.

Paul is not just turning our idea of Jesus upside down. He's turning our preconceptions about God himself upside down.

What's your preconception of God? A distant Creator? A harsh Judge? A cruel taskmaster? Look at Jesus in the cradle. Look at Jesus on the cross. And let him turn your view of God upside down.

Meditate

Since all he comes to ransom,
By all be he adored,
The infant born in Bethl'hem,
The Saviour and the Lord.

And idol forms shall perish,
And error shall decay,
And Christ shall wield his sceptre,
Our Lord and God for aye.

(From "A great and mighty wonder" by St Germanus, 634-734)

∽

Prayer

O Lord Jesus Christ,
draw thou our hearts unto thee;
join them together in inseparable love,
that we may abide in thee and thou in us,
and that the everlasting covenant between us
may stand sure for ever.
Let the fiery darts of thy love
pierce through all our slothful faculties and inward powers,
that we, being happily wounded,
may so become whole and sound.
Let us have no lover but thyself alone;
let us seek no joy nor comfort except in thee.
Amen.

(Myles Coverdale, Bishop of Exeter and Bible translator, 1488-1569)

Born as a servant

*"Rather, he made himself nothing by taking the very
nature of a servant."*
Philippians 2 v 7

Imagine the scene. Jesus and his disciples are sitting around the
meal table. Throughout the ebb and flow of conversation, they
all naturally look to him as their leader. After all, each one of them
is there because at some point they obeyed a call to follow him.
Plus he's demonstrated dramatic power over the past three years—
healing the sick, feeding the hungry, even raising the dead. And
although the way he talks about his plans has left the disciples
somewhat confused, they're certain he's heading for the throne.

And then Jesus leaves the meal table, takes off his cloak and wraps
a towel around his waist. The chatter soon fades as they watch in
stunned amazement. But when Jesus takes a bowl of water and
begins to wash their feet, the silence is punctuated by gasps.

It's hard to convey the shock of this moment or find a modern
parallel. Jesus was adopting the position of slave. Any travel along

the dusty roads of first-century Palestine left your feet dirty. So on arrival at your destination, a slave might wash your feet. The disciples, though, don't have access to a slave and so their feet have gone unwashed. Until now.

Peter's cry of protest captures the scandal of the moment: "No, you shall never wash my feet" (John 13 v 8). Only after the event does the apostle John begin to get it: "Having loved his own who were in the world," he comments in his Gospel, "he loved them to the end" (John 13 v 1).

No story from the life of Jesus better encapsulates the truth that Paul expresses in Philippians 2 v 7: "He made himself nothing by taking the very nature of a servant". Indeed, there are good reasons to suppose Paul might have had this story in mind. The word "servant" is literally "slave". Jesus assumed the role of a slave. Paul is talking about the whole of Jesus' life. Jesus submitted to the will of the Father, served the needs of his people and became obedient to death. But when he washed his disciples' feet in John 13, he quite literally took the role normally performed by a slave. He was very clearly demonstrating his servanthood.

Three things makes Jesus' actions all the more remarkable—three things John tells us that Jesus knew.

First, "Jesus knew that the hour had come for him to leave this world" (John 13 v 1). Even though Jesus knew he would die the following day, he served his disciples. Think of the excuses we make for not serving. "I've got a lot on my mind at the moment." No one could ever have said that with more justification than Jesus on the night before his death. But that was the night when he washes his disciples' feet.

Second, "Jesus knew that the Father had put all things under his power" (John 13 v 3). "I'll leave this to someone else," we might say. "I've got more important things to do." But not Jesus. He was the most important person in the universe. And yet he got up from the meal table and got down on his knees...

Third, "he knew who was going to betray him" (John 13 v 11). "I'm willing to serve," we might say, "but not that person—not after the way they've treated me". Yet Jesus washes the feet of Judas knowing that Judas already has 30 pieces of silver jangling in his wallet.

Take a moment to reflect on your excuses for not serving. How do they measure up against the example of the Lord Jesus?

∽

There's a twist in the story. After Jesus has washed their feet, he sits down and says this:

> *You call me "Teacher" and "Lord", and rightly so, for that is what I am. Now that I, your Lord and Teacher, have washed your feet, you also should wash one another's feet. I have set you an example that you should do as I have done for you. Very truly I tell you, no servant is greater than his master, nor is a messenger greater than the one who sent him. Now that you know these things, you will be blessed if you do them.* (John 13 v 13-17)

The life and death of Jesus are more than an example. Only Jesus is the Saviour. The world will not be saved by lots of people doing their best to be like Jesus. It's Jesus alone who saves his people (as we shall see).

But make no mistake: the life and death of Jesus are an example. And, though it feels counter-intuitive, servanthood turns out to be the way of blessing—the way to true happiness and wholeness.

Think about the Christians you know who are most preoccupied with themselves, their desires, their status. And then think about the Christians you know who are most preoccupied with serving others and with God's glory. Who are the happiest?

Jesus willingly made himself a slave in order to make you clean. And now he says to his followers, *Do you want to have a really happy Christmas? Fetch a bowl and a towel, get down on your knees, and follow my example.*

Meditate
Blessed are the poor in spirit,
for theirs is the kingdom of heaven.
Blessed are those who mourn,
for they will be comforted.
Blessed are the meek,
for they will inherit the earth.
Blessed are those who hunger
and thirst for righteousness,
for they will be filled.
(Matthew 5 v 3-6)

~♭

Prayer
Give us grace to endeavour after a truly Christian spirit
to seek to attain that temper of forbearance and patience
of which our blessed Saviour has set us the highest example;
and which, while it prepares us for the spiritual happiness of the life to come,
will secure to us the best enjoyment of what this world can give. Amen.
(Jane Austen, author, 1775-1817)

Born as the divine servant

"Rather, he made himself nothing by taking the very nature of a servant."
Philippians 2 v 7

There's a lot that the movie *Bruce Almighty* gets wrong about God (played by Morgan Freeman). But this it gets right: whenever we see God in the movie, he's cleaning floors. And whenever we see God in the pages of human history, he looks like Jesus—the Jesus who washes feet.

Jesus "made himself nothing". It's literally "he emptied himself". Christ Jesus "did not consider equality with God something to be used to his own advantage," according to verse 6. It's literally "a thing to be grasped" (ESV). Now Paul describes Jesus going a step further. Instead of grasping, he let go. Instead of tightening his grip on the advantages of his deity, he came to earth at the first Christmas with an open hand. Instead of pulling his majesty tightly around himself, he took off his glory to become a servant.

Some people have taken the idea of Jesus emptying himself and pushed it hard—too hard. They claim that Jesus emptied himself of some aspects of his deity. He gave up being all-knowing, all-powerful and all-present. In effect he stopped being fully divine. (For the record, this is known as the "kenotic" view of Christ, which comes from the Greek word Paul uses here for "emptying": *kenosis*.)

But elsewhere Paul says, "In Christ all the fullness of the Deity lives in bodily form" (Colossians 2 v 9). Far from being emptied of divinity, Jesus was *full* of divinity.

In fact, Paul doesn't say what exactly Jesus emptied himself *of*. That's a clue that he's probably speaking metaphorically. But Paul does tell us clearly what it actually meant for Jesus to empty himself: he did it "by taking the very nature of a servant". In effect, Jesus emptied himself not by *losing* something, but by *gaining* something—servanthood. In the process, of course, he lost the advantages of divine majesty and security. Jesus emptied himself by adding rejection, hostility, pain, thirst, betrayal and shame.

In October AD 451 leaders of the church met at the Council of Chalcedon to thrash out what it means to say that Jesus is both divine and human. The council rejected the ideas that Jesus stopped being fully God, or that Jesus only *appeared* to be human, or that the divine and human mingled to create some kind of hybrid nature. Instead, they said Jesus was one person with "two natures, inconfusedly, unchangeably, indivisibly, inseparably". Decisive to the outcome was a letter by the pope Leo the Great. Leo said that at the incarnation, "lowliness was assumed by majesty, weakness by power, mortality by eternity … enriching what was human, not impairing what was divine". This is the person we worship—fully God and fully man, each without compromising either.

Everyone knew a slave had no rights. What Jesus lost at that first Christmas was the enjoyment of the rights of a deity. He had the right to be worshipped, but he accepted rejection. He had the right to glory, but he accepted shame. He had the right to exercise power, but he chose the path of weakness. When he did exercise his divine power, it was always for the benefit for others. Jesus is always fully divine, but during his time on earth he chose not to use the privileges of his divine sonship.

So Jesus didn't swap the nature of God for the nature of a servant. Instead, the nature of God took on the form of a servant. The Reformer John Calvin says:

> Here is something marvellous: the Son of God descended
> from heaven in such a way that, without leaving heaven,
> he willed to be borne in the virgin's womb, to go about
> the earth, and to hang upon the cross; yet he continuously
> filled the world even as he had done from the beginning!
> (*Institutes*, 2.13.4)

And that's the point. What we see at Christmas is the servanthood of God. And it takes our breath away. We assume that being God is all about power and pomp. And, of course, God is all-powerful. He can do whatever he wants. Nothing and no one can constrain or restrain his power. But God doesn't use his power for grandstanding or ego trips. God uses his power in love. God uses his power to serve his people.

What authority do you have? In the workplace? In the home? In the church? In what situations are you physically stronger or more capable? In what areas does your knowledge and experience give you the edge?

There's nothing wrong with authority. We don't need to be hesitant about rightly exercising power. The question is: *Do you use your power like Jesus? Do you use it for the sake of others? Have you taken on the nature of a servant?* Jesus himself said:

> *Whoever wants to become great among you must be your servant, and whoever wants to be first must be slave of all. For even the Son of Man did not come to be served, but to serve, and to give his life as a ransom for many.* (Mark 10 v 43-45)

If you want to draw near to God, then clean floors with him.

Meditate
A great and mighty wonder, a full and holy cure!
The Virgin bears the Infant with virgin-honour pure.
The Word becomes incarnate and yet remains on high!
And cherubim sing anthems to shepherds from the sky.
(From "A great and mighty wonder" by St Germanus, 634-734)

∽

Prayer
Lord, make me an instrument of your peace.
Where there is hatred, let me sow love;
where there is injury, pardon; where there is doubt, faith;
where there is despair, hope; where there is darkness, light;
where there is sadness, joy;
O Divine Master, grant that I may not so much
seek to be consoled as to console;
to be understood as to understand; to be loved as to love.
For it is in giving that we receive;
it is in pardoning that we are pardoned;
and it is in dying that we are born to eternal life.
(Francis of Assisi, 1181-1226)

Born as the new Adam

10

"… being made in human likeness."
Philippians 2 v 7

I'm not a fan of costume parties. I have enough trouble retaining my dignity without throwing it away in a pathetic attempt to look like Elvis.

When we talk about someone being "like Elvis", we don't mean they *are* Elvis. We mean they look like Elvis—white jumpsuit, dark glasses, stick-on sideburns. Perhaps they sound like Elvis too. But no one would be fooled into thinking Elvis had returned by my attempts to impersonate him.

Is this what Paul means when he says Christ Jesus was made "in human likeness"? Does this mean Jesus was merely *like* a human being without *really* being human? Was Jesus a human-impersonator?

The answer is *No*. Jesus was truly human.

So why does Paul say "made in human likeness" rather than simply "made human"? One reason is to rule out any sense that

Jesus turned from God into man (leaving his divinity behind). The fifth-century church father Theodoret said, "The words *in the likeness of men* are appropriate, for the nature that he assumed was truly human, and yet he was not merely a man."

∽

But there may be another reason why Paul says "in human likeness", and to see it we need to rewind to the beginning of the Bible story. Genesis 5 v 1-3 says:

> *When God created mankind, he made them in the likeness of God. He created them male and female and blessed them. And he named them "Mankind" when they were created. When Adam had lived 130 years, he had a son in his own likeness, in his own image; and he named him Seth.*

The first man, Adam, had a son "in his own likeness". In other words, a human being reproduced another human being. Adam didn't produce a dog. The point of the word "likeness" is not that Seth merely *appeared* to be human. The point is that he was as human as Adam.

And that's Paul's point in Philippians 2. Jesus was as human as Adam.

∽

But the word "likeness" is not only used of Seth in Genesis 5. Genesis 5 also tells us that God made all mankind "in the likeness of God". This time the word "likeness" doesn't mean that human beings are as divine as God. It means we were made in God's image to reflect his glory in his world (Genesis 1 v 26-28). We were made to rule God's world—in the image of the sovereign God. And we were made to live in community—in the image of the communal, three-in-one God. We were made to be like God.

This makes our rebellion against God all the more astonishing and tragic. In the Garden of Eden the snake said that if humanity broke God's command, then they would "be like God, knowing good and evil" (Genesis 3 v 5). They were seduced by the promise of being like God—even though they were *already* like God.

In trying to be like God, humanity became less like God. The image of God in humanity was marred and spoilt.

∽

Let's put all these pieces together. What does Paul mean when he says Christ Jesus was "made in human likeness"? He means that he was truly human. But, for those who pick up the echoes of Genesis, Paul is also saying so much more than this.

Paul has already told us that Christ Jesus "did not count equality with God a thing to be grasped" (v 6, ESV). But that is precisely what the first Adam *did* attempt; he tried to grasp equality with God. He tried to become "like God". Not "like God" in the way God intended—ruling over creation in love and enjoying a relationship with God. Adam tried to be like God by determining for himself good and evil. He wanted to be god in the place of God.

Enter Jesus. Jesus is the new Adam, the true Adam. He is humanity as humanity was intended to be. He doesn't grasp at divinity. Instead, as we've seen, he submits to the Father and uses his power to serve.

Through Adam, humanity lost its way. In fact, we didn't just wander off course. We resolutely turned around and headed in the wrong direction. In Jesus, humanity is put back on track. And Christmas is the first landmark along that road.

The challenge to us is: *Will we join Jesus?* Will *we* change direction? That's the big choice we made when we first became a Christian. But it's also the choice we make again and again whenever we face temptation—in that moment, will you follow Adam and decide for yourself what is "right" for you, or will you follow Jesus in doing what God says is right?

You will face temptation today. But will you follow Jesus?

Meditate

Adam's likeness, Lord, efface,
Stamp thy image in its place;
Second Adam from above,
Reinstate us in thy Love.
Let us thee, tho' lost, regain,
Thee, the Life, the Inner Man:
O, to all thyself impart,
Form'd in each believing heart.

(From "Hark the herald angels sing" by Charles Wesley, 1707-1788)

Prayer

Our first father, Adam,
tumbled down himself
from a most excellent and high
and honourable estate
into the mire of misery
and deep sea of shame and mischief.
But, O Christ, thou,
putting forth thine hand,
did raise humanity up.
Even so we, unless we be lifted up by thee,
shall lie still for ever.
O good Christ, our most gracious Redeemer,
grant that, as thou dost mercifully
now raise up this my body [from sleep],
so, I beseech thee, raise up my mind and heart
to the light of the true knowledge of the love of thee,
that my conversation may be in heaven,
where thou art.
Amen.

(John Bradford, English Reformer and martyr, 1510-1555)

Born as the true man

"And being found in appearance as a man..."
Philippians 2 v 8

There may well be moments this Christmas when you feel as if no one understands. "The turkey is overcooked," someone says—without appreciating all the hard work you've put into preparing the meal. "I would have preferred it in blue," someone murmurs—without appreciating all the hours you spent struggling through the crowds of Christmas shoppers. "Having the house full of visitors drives me crazy," someone complains—but you'll be spending Christmas day on your own, grieving a relationship that was or a relationship that might have been.

"No one appreciates me; no one understands," we think. But this verse tells us that isn't true.

∾

Jesus was "found in appearance as a man," says verse 8. As we've already seen, Paul is not saying Jesus only *appeared* to be human, whereas in fact he was something else underneath. Jesus wasn't wearing a disguise. He wasn't all show without real substance underneath. At a time when many people doubted Christ's humanity, Paul's point was that Jesus was *recognised* to be a man. Those who knew him well "found" or discovered that he was truly human. In other words, the humanity of Jesus is not simply a blind assertion. We don't make Jesus human by shouting it loudly. No, Paul's point is that all the evidence was there in the life of Jesus.

Consider what Luke says about the childhood of Jesus: "Jesus grew in wisdom and stature, and in favour with God and man" (Luke 2 v 52). Although the divine nature of Jesus continued to be all-knowing, in some mysterious way his human nature gained wisdom. He learnt from experience. And Jesus grew in size. Perhaps, like so many families, Joseph and Mary measured the growth of their children with notches on the doorpost. There's one mark labelled "Jesus, aged 5". Then a few inches up, "Jesus, aged 8". Growing limbs and muscles is a hard trick to pull off if you're only pretending to be human!

There's a telling similarity between Luke's description of the childhood of John the Baptist and the childhood of Jesus: John "grew and became strong in spirit" (1 v 80), and Jesus "grew and became strong" (2 v 40). Luke's point is that Jesus grew as a child in the same way that John grew as a child.

Or consider what those who knew Jesus well made of him. In the Gospels we get an account of three years of Jesus' life. But his family knew him for 30 years. With this in mind, consider Mark 3 v 20-21:

> *Then Jesus entered a house, and again a crowd gathered, so that he and his disciples were not even able to eat. When his family heard about this, they went to take charge of him, for they said, "He is out of his mind."*

When his family hear what Jesus is saying and doing, they assume he's gone crazy. And that's not the conclusion you come to if think someone was never truly human. It's striking that what prompts them to doubt his sanity is the fact that he's not eating. Perhaps Jesus had always had a good appetite. Something must be wrong if he's not eating, they think. Perhaps you can imagine that kind of interaction going on in your family! For 30 years Jesus had eaten with them, worked with them, played with them, slept with them, joked with them. As a result, although his family had doubts about whether he was the Messiah, they never doubted he was human.

If Jesus was simply disguised as a human being, then it was a very good disguise! He grew like a human, looked like a human, talked like a human, ate like a human, grew tired like a human, suffered like a human. He felt grief and cried like a human. This was no mere disguise. The explanation that best fits the facts is that Jesus was truly human—as human as you and I.

∾

And he didn't stop being human after his death and resurrection. On the first Easter Day the disciples couldn't quite believe that Jesus was alive—it all seemed too good to be true. So Jesus asked for something to eat. "They gave him a piece of broiled fish, and he took it and ate it in their presence" (Luke 24 v 42-43). They were not seeing a ghost. The risen Jesus was still really human.

And Jesus is still human now that he's ascended into heaven.

Therefore, since we have a great high priest who has ascended into heaven, Jesus the Son of God, let us hold firmly to the faith we profess. For we do not have a high priest who is unable to feel sympathy for our weaknesses. (Hebrews 4 v 14-15)

The one who ascended into heaven is the one who lay in the manger. Our high priest before God is the one who shared our weaknesses. Jesus knows what it's like to be human because he *was* human and *still is* human—as human as you are. The only difference is that now his humanity is *enlarged* by his glory. Now by the Spirit he can sympathise with every one of us everywhere. And that means we can "approach God's throne of grace with confidence" (Hebrews 4 v 16). When it feels as if no one else understands us, we can come to one who truly does. When we feel alone in our weariness and weakness, we can come to God's throne of grace in prayer. When our hearts ache for what we have lost, we can bring that emotion to the one who has felt it too.

But Christ didn't just became human so he could sympathise with us as we struggle and suffer. He came to save, heal and transform. He became one with us so that we might become one with him, and so share his relationship with the Father. Listen to John Calvin:

> Who could have done this had not the self-same Son of God become the Son of man, and had not so taken what was ours as to impart what was his to us, and to make what was his by nature ours by grace? Therefore relying on this pledge, we trust that we are sons of God, for God's natural Son fashioned for himself a body from our body, flesh from our flesh, bones from our bones, that he might be one with us. Ungrudgingly he took our nature upon himself to *impart to us what was his*, and to become both Son of God and Son of Man in common with us.
>
> (Calvin's *Institutes*, 2.12.2)

Meditate

Our God, heav'n cannot hold him,
Nor earth sustain;
Heav'n and earth shall flee away
When he comes to reign.
In the bleak mid-winter
A stable place sufficed,
The Lord God Almighty—
Jesus Christ.

(From "In the bleak mid-winter" by Christina Rossetti, 1830-1894)

᭡

Prayer

O Lord, thou who hast said,
thou wilt not break the bruised reed,
nor quench the smoking flax.
Be merciful, we beseech thee, unto all those who,
through fear and weakness,
have denied thee by their hypocrisy.
May it please thee to strengthen their weak knees—
thou who art the strength of them that stand—
and to lift up their feeble hands,
that their little smoke may increase into a great flame,
and their bruised reed into a mighty oak,
able to abide all the blustering blasts
and stormy tempests of adversity.
Amen.

(John Bradford, English Reformer and martyr, 1510-1555)

Born in humility

12

"He humbled himself…"
Philippians 2 v 8

How do I look?

We live in an age in which we constantly worry about how other people perceive us. "How do I look?" is one of our culture's catchphrases.

And no wonder. A couple of generations ago your identity was pretty much handed to you at birth. The chances were you would do the job your parents did and live in the area in which they lived. Today, social mobility means most of us have the freedom to invent and reinvent ourselves. That's a great blessing. But it brings with it a greater level of anxiety. If my identity is down to me, then I can easily end up evaluating my performance all the time. If my identity can be remade from one week to the next, then who I am is constantly up for grabs. Social media amplify these anxieties. When I post a photo on Facebook, "How do I look?" is not just addressed to the people in the room, but to the whole world—and I desperately want them to give me their "thumbs up". So how do we cope?

~

Christ Jesus "humbled himself," says Paul in verse 8. It's not the first time Paul has talked about humility in this chapter. Back in verses 3-4 he said:

> *Do nothing out of selfish ambition or vain conceit. Rather, in humility value others above yourselves, not looking to your own interests but each of you to the interests of the others.*

Think about your interaction with social media. Evaluate it against the criteria of "selfish ambition" and "vain conceit". How does it measure up?

The alternative is humility. "Rather, in humility value others above yourselves," says Paul.

But true humility is not found by pretending you're worse than you really are. "Thank you for your contribution," someone says, and we reply, "It was nothing. I didn't really know what I was doing". I'm British—and we do self-deprecation in spades. But really it's just an attempt to *appear* humble. And appearance is key. We're still worried about what people think of us—and we don't want them to think we're full of ourselves.

Instead, the measure of genuine humility is not so much what you think about yourself, but what you think about others. When you meet a humble person, you don't come away thinking, "What a humble person". You come away thinking, "That person was really interested in me". Or, as Paul puts it, humility is expressed by "not looking to your own interests but … to the interests of the others".

"How do I look?" By looking away from yourself.

~

But we do like to look at ourselves. Flick through any set of photos and I guarantee you'll pause at the ones which have you in them.

The key to genuine humility is to look at Jesus. Jesus is the model for our humility. Think of Jesus in the manger. Not for him a palace or a royal bed. Think of Jesus welcoming children. Children were of no importance in the culture of his day, but Jesus overrode the protests of his disciples to welcome children. Or think of Jesus touching the leper—risking his cleanliness to cleanse the outcast. Think of the woman who gatecrashed a Pharisee's party to wash the feet of Jesus. Jesus' reputation was on the line, but still he let her wipe his feet with her tears.

Ultimately though, "he humbled himself by becoming obedient to death" (v 8). He submitted to trumped-up charges and unjust justice. He let the soldiers mock him and scourge his back. He allowed himself to be nailed between two criminals.

"When they hurled their insults at him, he did not retaliate," says 1 Peter 2 v 23. "When he suffered, he made no threats. Instead, he entrusted himself to him who judges justly." Jesus' confidence in his Father's approval meant he never needed to assert it. A thief grasps at things they do not own. By contrast, Jesus "did not count equality with God a thing to be grasped" (v 6, ESV) because he was secure in his Father's love.

And it can be the same for us. True humility is recognising who we are without Christ and who we are *in Christ*. Without Christ, we are sinners heading for hell. It's hard to be full of yourself when you realise you're full of sin. But in Christ, we are children of God. In Christ, we have the Father's full approval. And the way people treat you cannot change that.

∽

We all want to be the star of the show. But hardly anyone is watching. Everyone else is too busy with their own performances. Meanwhile Jesus invites us to play a role in the greatest story ever told. This Christmas, let's learn our lines and play our part in the story of Jesus.

Here are some of the reviews of his performance. "He has done everything well" (Mark 7 v 37). "To him who sits on the throne and to the Lamb be praise and honour and glory and power, for ever and ever!" (Revelation 5 v 13). "The name that is above every name" (Philippians 2 v 9). We don't need to crave the applause of other people; we can enjoy the applause that Christ has earned. Why would you want to be part of any other story?

Meditate

Him the angels all adored,
Their maker and their king;
Tidings of their humbled Lord
They now to mortals bring.
Emptied of his majesty,
Of his dazzling glories shorn,
Being's Source begins to be,
And God himself is born!

See the eternal Son of God
A mortal Son of Man;
Dwelling in an earthly clod,
Whom Heav'n cannot contain!
Stand amazed, ye heavens, at this!
See the Lord of earth and skies
Humbled to the dust he is,
And in a manger lies!

(From "Glory be to God on high" by Charles Wesley, 1707-1788)

~ᴗ

Prayer

Almighty and everlasting God,
who, of thy tender love towards mankind,
hast sent thy Son our Saviour Jesus Christ
to take upon him our flesh,
and to suffer death upon the cross,
that all mankind should follow
the example of his great humility:
Mercifully grant that we
may both follow the example of his patience,
and also be made partakers of his resurrection;
through the same Jesus Christ our Lord,
who liveth and reigneth with thee
and the Holy Spirit, one God,
for ever and ever.
Amen.

(The Book of Common Prayer)

Born to die

"… by becoming obedient to death"
Philippians 2 v 8

There's a famous Middle-Eastern fable about a servant who is sent by his master on an errand to the market. In the bustle of the marketplace the servant turns to see Death. As their eyes meet, Death makes a gesture towards him. Certain that Death is pursuing him, the terrified servant races back home. He begs his master to lend him a horse so that he can ride to Samarra to escape Death. The master gives the servant the use of a horse, and moments later the servant is riding as fast as he can along the Samarra road.

Meanwhile, the master goes to the market, where he too sees Death. "Why did you make a threatening gesture to my servant this morning?" he asks. "Oh no," replies Death. "That wasn't a threatening gesture. I was merely surprised to see him here, for I have an appointment with him tonight in Samarra."

The point, of course, is that none of us can escape the Grim Reaper. People used to say that there were two certainties in life—death and taxes. Now, however, it seems that off-shore tax-avoidance schemes enable some people to escape taxes! But no one escapes death—not in the end. Cryonic freezing cannot help us. No one has been born who is not subject to the authority of death.

No one, that is, except Jesus.

⌒

"The wages of sin is death," says Paul in Romans 6 v 23. But Jesus never sinned. He was the one person in the whole of human history who didn't deserve to die. Death had no claim on him. When death called, he could have ignored it.

It's not just that there was no sin in Jesus. There was life in him. "For as the Father has life in himself," says Jesus in John 5 v 26, "so he has granted the Son also to have life in himself". Jesus contained within himself more than enough life to overcome death. "I am the resurrection and the life," he told a grieving sister (John 11 v 25). And then he proved it by raising her brother, Lazarus, from the dead.

⌒

And yet Paul says that Jesus became obedient to death. Jesus submitted to its claim and answered its call. Some words of Jesus himself help us to make sense of this. In John 10 he says:

> *I am the good shepherd. The good shepherd lays down his life for the sheep … The reason my Father loves me is that I lay down my life—only to take it up again. No one takes it from me, but I lay it down of my own accord.* (John 10 v 11, 17-18)

The religious leaders handed Jesus over to be executed. Pilate passed the order for execution. The Roman soldiers nailed him to a cross. But at any point Jesus could have stepped away from the cross or called down an army of angels. Death did not take his life from him. Jesus chose to lay down his life for his sheep.

~

The birth of a baby is a beautiful thing. The new life that has been growing in the womb comes into the world. So much promise and potential are cradled in a mother's arms.

The birth of Jesus was no different. When Mary and Joseph presented their newborn son at the temple, Simeon took Jesus in his arms and praised God. "For my eyes have seen your salvation," he said (Luke 2 v 30). So much promise and potential in his arms. All the promises of God coming together in this baby—but not in the way these new parents expect.

Because then Simeon turned to Mary and said, "And a sword will pierce your own soul too" (Luke 2 v 35). It's a cryptic remark to be sure. But it seems to be a hint that Mary's heart would be broken. This son would not live to bury his mother. Instead, Mary would watch her son be crucified. Even as the Christmas scene is played out on stage, death is loitering in the wings.

Jesus was born to die. But his death was not the inevitable end of another human life. Still less was it the tragic climax of a misguided venture. It was part of a plan. And it was part of that plan from the beginning. We'll see why in the next chapter. But we've already had a hint in the words of Jesus: "The good shepherd lays down his life for the sheep" (John 10 v 11).

Perhaps death lurks close to you this Christmas. Perhaps your prognosis is bad. Perhaps this will be your first Christmas after the death of a loved one, and their absence feels as powerful as their presence once did. You are not alone. Jesus, too, has faced the reality of death. And it was not the end of the story…

Meditate

The holly bears a berry,
As red as any blood,
And Mary bore sweet Jesus Christ
For to do us sinners good.
The holly bears a prickle,
As sharp as any thorn,
And Mary bore sweet Jesus Christ
On Christmas Day in the morn.
The holly bears a bark,
As bitter as any gall,
And Mary bore sweet Jesus Christ
For to redeem us all.
(From "The holly and the ivy", traditional English carol)

∽

Prayer

It is a thing most wonderful,
Almost too wonderful to be,
That God's own Son should come from heaven,
And die to save a child like me.
It is most wonderful to know
His love for me so free and sure;
But 'tis more wonderful to see
My love for him so faint and poor.
And yet I want to love thee, Lord;
O light the flame within my heart,
And I will love thee more and more,
Until I see thee as thou art.
(William Walsham How, 1823-1897)

Born to die for us

"… by becoming obedient to death"
Philippians 2 v 8

Imagine you get a Christmas card in the post. It's a typical nativity scene: Jesus in the manger, Mary, Joseph, the shepherds, the Magi, a donkey perhaps, and the Grim Reaper.

The Grim Reaper?! What's he doing there? That's not the tone we want. We don't like to think about death, and certainly not at Christmas. But, as we saw in the last chapter, death is a brooding presence in the background of the Christmas story.

Just ask the mothers of Bethlehem. The Magi unwittingly tip King Herod off that a new king has arrived on the scene. So Herod orders the execution of all the baby boys of Bethlehem (Matthew 2 v 13-18). Jesus only escapes because God tells Joseph in a dream to flee with his family to Egypt.

It's a powerful reminder that Jesus is not always welcome in our world. This earth is disputed territory. Humanity is under the power of Satan. And so Jesus is born into a battle. He's come to take on a foe. Bethlehem quickly becomes the battlefield. And this will be a battle to the death.

∽

Here's an explanation of Christmas that doesn't often make it into carol services:

> *Since the children have flesh and blood, [Jesus] too shared in*
> *their humanity so that by his death he might break the power*
> *of him who holds the power of death—that is, the devil—and*
> *free those who all their lives were held in slavery by their fear of*
> *death.* (Hebrews 2 v 14-15)

This is why Jesus took on flesh and blood—so that he might break the power of Satan and set us free from death.

What is the power of Satan and the slavery of death? It is that all who sin against God deserve to die—and that, of course, includes you. Death is the penalty of sin. In the Garden of Eden, humanity switched sides. We rejected God and joined Satan in his rebellion. And that set us on a course that inevitably leads to death.

But at the first Christmas Jesus took on our flesh and blood. He shared our humanity so that he might bear the penalty of death in our place—"that by his death he might break … the power of death". Justice demands death as the penalty for sin. But justice cannot and will not demand a double payment. When Jesus dies in our place, our penalty is paid and we walk free. By his death Jesus writes across our charge sheet, "Paid in full".

This was a battle to the death, and Jesus paid the price. He became obedient to death.

∽

But death was not the end for Jesus. In dying Jesus conquered death. Once the price had been paid—as it was at the cross—death had no further claim on him. Nor does it have any claim on us. And so he rose again. And we rise again in him.

This was a battle to the death, and in the end it was death itself which lay defeated on the battlefield.

~

It's easy to default to a very sanitised version of Christmas. Our Christmas cards show the baby sleeping soundly in the manger, and everything is cute, clean and charming. But Jesus came to die on a cross. The cross wasn't some accident of history. It was the *climax* of history. It was the climax of *eternity*. The implication of Philippians 2 v 6 is that Jesus made a calculation in eternity, an eternal decision, to leave the glory and safety of heaven to come to earth, to come to the cross. And that wasn't simply a romantic gesture. He came because the cradle and the cross were the only way to save us from the judgment we deserve.

Here we see the cost of our grumbling and arguing. We talk about Jesus dying for our sins, yet we often think of those sins in rather abstract terms. But he died for the sins *you* commit—the one you think of as "big sins" and the ones you think of as "small sins". The cross of Jesus reveals the true character of our little foibles. Look underneath the charms of temptation and you discover the rotten corpse of death.

But the cross also reveals the true extent of God's love to us. Jesus died for your sins. When he heard you grumbling and arguing, he didn't turn away in disgust. In his love he turned towards the cross, arms opened wide to take the nails. And now in his love he turns towards you, arms opened wide to embrace you.

Meditate

Hark, a voice from yonder manger,
Soft and sweet, doth entreat: "Flee from woe and danger!
Brethren come, from all doth grieve you,
You are freed; all you need I will surely give you."

Come, then, let us hasten yonder;
Here let all, great and small, kneel in awe and wonder.
Love him who with love is yearning.
Hail the star that from far bright with hope is burning.
(From "All my heart this night rejoices" by Paul Gerhardt, 1607-1676)

~૭

Prayer

Our Father,
we pray that out of your glorious riches
you may strengthen us with power
through your Spirit in our inner being,
so that Christ may dwell in our hearts through faith.
We pray this so that we,
being rooted and established in love,
may have power,
together with all the your holy people,
to grasp how wide and long and high and deep
is the love of Christ,
and to know this love that surpasses knowledge—
that we may be filled
to the measure of all your fulness.
Amen.
(Adapted from Ephesians 3 v 16-19)

Born to die in shame

"… even death on a cross!"
Philippians 2 v 8

On 1 July 1916, in the middle of the Battle of the Somme, a box of hand grenades slipped into a trench crowded with British soldiers. As the grenades fell, the pins of two of them were dislodged. Billy McFadzean, a 20-year-old soldier with the Royal Irish Rifles, threw himself on top of the grenades. He was killed instantly. But he saved his comrades. Because of his sacrifice no one else was killed and only one other soldier was injured. His citation for bravery read:

> Private McFadzean, instantly realising the danger to his
> comrades, with heroic courage threw himself on the
> top of the bombs. The bombs exploded blowing him
> to pieces, but only one other man was injured. He well
> knew his danger, being himself a bomber, but without a
> moment's hesitation he gave his life for his comrades.

The following year McFadzean's father was presented by King George V with his son's Victoria Cross, the British Army's highest award for bravery.

There is no shame in death—in fact, most of us admire a noble end like that. Many deaths, like that of Billy McFadzean, have involved "heroic courage".

∽

But there was nothing honourable about crucifixion. No one looked on with admiration. The flow of verses 7-8 makes this clear.

> *He made himself nothing*
> > *by taking the very nature of a servant,*
> > *being made in human likeness,*
> *And being found in appearance as a man,*
> > *he humbled himself*
> > *by becoming obedient to death—*
> > *even death on a cross!*

Jesus took four steps down as he humbled himself.

- Step 1: He became a servant.

- Step 2: He appeared as a man.

- Step 3: He became obedient to death.

And you might think there was nowhere else to go. How can you go lower than death? But Jesus had not finished humbling himself.

- Step 4: Even death on the cross.

The word "even" is the giveaway. Death on a cross was both horrific and humiliating. But "even" this was what Jesus accepted.

Crucifixion was a particularly cruel form of execution. It was basically death by torture. And you were lifted up so that all your humiliations were on display. It was reserved only for the worst of criminals and could never be inflicted on a Roman citizen. The Roman politician and philosopher Cicero said, "Let the very name of the cross be far away not only from the body of a Roman citizen, but even from his thoughts, his eyes, his ears."

By embracing the cross, Jesus not only accepted death—he died in shame. The supreme moment of Christ's servanthood and humility was the cross.

∾

Before we turn away in horror and disgust, listen to Paul: "God demonstrates his own love for us in this: while we were still sinners, Christ died for us" (Romans 5 v 8). This is the measure of the love of God. This is how far Christ will go to save us: "Even death on a cross".

It's very easy for us to look at our sin and feel ashamed. It's easy for us to see our weaknesses and feel worthless. And then we wonder whether God really loves us.

Or perhaps we view his love in a formal kind of way. God forgives us, but we find it hard to imagine that he takes any delight in us. Perhaps we think that at best he tolerates us.

But here is the measure of his love: "Even death on a cross".

∾

When Adam and Eve were first made, we're told that "Adam and his wife were both naked, and they felt no shame" (Genesis 2 v 25). But the very first thing that happens after they reject God is that they realise they are naked and try to cover themselves with fig leaves. So God in his kindness makes clothes for them from animal skins. It's the first time something dies in the Bible's story. An animal dies to hide human shame.

Ever since then, our fear of nakedness has become a sign of our deep, inner shame. We fear exposing our bodies to others because we can't trust what they might say or do. And we fear exposing our inner selves to others because we can't trust what they might say or do.

As they prepared him for crucifixion, the Roman soldiers took Jesus' clothes from him and shared them out by casting lots (Mark 15 v 24). Jesus died naked, exposed, shamed.

But just as the animal died to clothe Adam and Eve, so Jesus died to clothe us in his righteousness. And so we have no reason to feel ashamed when we come before God, because Jesus has taken our shame.

In the end, the death of Jesus *was* truly heroic. Despite all the insults he heard as he hung there, and all the degradations he experienced, his death was victorious. He defeated death, removed our guilt and covered our shame.

What are you hiding this Christmas? What's your secret shame? What's the thing you hope no one else will ever uncover? You don't need to hide it from Jesus. You don't need to feel ashamed. Bring it to the One who bore all our shame and suffering on the cross.

Meditate

Man of Sorrows! What a name
For the Son of God, who came
Ruined sinners to reclaim:
Hallelujah, what a Saviour!

Bearing shame and scoffing rude,
In my place condemned he stood,
Sealed my pardon with his blood:
Hallelujah, what a Saviour!

(From "Man of sorrows! What a name" by Philip Paul Bliss, 1838-1876)

∼

Prayer

O Christ, clothe me with thine own self,
that I may be so far from making provision
for my flesh to fulfil the lusts of it,
that I may quite put off all my carnal desires,
and crucify the kingdom of the flesh in me.
Be thou unto me a garment
to warm me from catching the cold of this world …
Put upon me as the elect of God,
mercy, meekness, love and peace.
Amen.

(John Bradford, Reformer and martyr, 1510-1555)

Born to die under God's curse

"… even death on a cross!"
Philippians 2 v 8

I wonder if you've ever been accused of eating or drinking too much. Christmas is a time when most of us overindulge.

It seems it was an accusation often levelled against Jesus too. Jesus liked sharing a meal and joining a party. Too much so, according to the religious leaders of his day. Jesus once said, "The Son of Man came eating and drinking, and you say, 'Here is a glutton and a drunkard, a friend of tax collectors and sinners'" (Luke 7 v 34).

What really scandalised the religious leaders was who Jesus chose to sit down at table with. Eating with someone was a sign that you accepted them—and Jesus ate with notorious sinners and tax collectors (who collaborated with the Gentile Roman government, who had desecrated God's land).

Does Jesus deny the Pharisees' accusation? No—he confirms it! In fact, the next thing that happens is that Jesus accepts the attentions of a sinful woman at a party by letting her wash his feet with her tears (Luke 7 v 36-50). Jesus was embodying God's grace. God welcomes his enemies—the very people who have lived their lives pushing him away. But the religious leaders didn't like this talk of grace. They worked hard to preserve their social standing through their outward acts of "righteousness": grace turned it upside down.

∾

After recalling this accusation, Jesus adds a rather cryptic remark: "But wisdom is proved right by all her children" (Luke 7 v 35). The accusation that Jesus is a glutton and a drunkard is an allusion to Deuteronomy 21 v 21, which describes how a rebellious, drunken son is to be stoned. The religious leaders are accusing Jesus of being just such a rebellious son. In response Jesus says in effect, *Time will tell who are the children of rebellion and who are the children of wisdom.*

It's not Jesus who is a rebellious son. Indeed, he will prove to be a faithful son—*the* faithful son—of Israel. It's Israel itself which is a son of rebellion.

And yet who is it that dies the death of a rebellious son? The passage in Deuteronomy which condemns a rebellious son also declares that anyone who hangs on a pole is cursed (21 v 22-23). Jesus is not the rebellious son. I am. You are. But it's Jesus who died under a curse. My curse. Your curse.

For first-century Jews, crucifixion wasn't just a shameful death. It was an accursed death. It was a public declaration that you were under the curse of God. No wonder Paul says, "*Even* death on a cross"! No one could have anticipated this: the Son of God under the curse of God.

∾

Let's rewind once more to the Garden of Eden. No sooner had God made the first man and woman than he blessed them:

> *God blessed them and said to them, "Be fruitful and increase in number; fill the earth and subdue it. Rule over the fish in the sea and the birds in the sky and over every living creature that moves on the ground."*　　　　　(Genesis 1 v 28)

But with humanity's rebellion, that blessing turns to curse. God said to Adam:

> *Cursed is the ground because of you;*
> *　through painful toil you will eat food from it*
> *　all the days of your life …*
> *For dust you are*
> *　and to dust you will return.*　　　(Genesis 3 v 17, 19)

Ever since, human life has been characterised by struggle, futility, fragility and death. In one way or another, we all feel the curse. Every twinge of pain, every harsh word heard, every disappointed hope is a sign of the curse. We're all heading for the fate of rebellious children—death.

Enter Jesus, the second Adam and the faithful son. He died the death of a rebellious child to absorb our curse and set us free. "Christ redeemed us from the curse of the law," says Paul in Galatians 3 v 13, "by becoming a curse for us, for it is written: 'Cursed is everyone who is hung on a pole.'"

∽

There will be happy times and sad times this Christmas—times when we feel the blessing of God and times when we feel the curse. Through Christ, Christians have been set free from God's curse on us personally—but we still live in a world that is under God's curse for sin generally. But now we look forward to a day when God will renew creation and set it free from its bondage to sin and decay.

So as we wait for that day, let us:

- **Receive the joys of God's blessings with gratitude.** At Christmas we experience so much of what is "good" in God's creation: music and dancing, sumptuous food, roaring laughter, nostalgic holiday movies, the warmth of human friendship. Thank God for each blessing you'll enjoy this Christmas.

- **Bear the pains of God's curse with hope.** At Christmas we will also experience something of God's curse on creation: dull aches, blazing rows or lonely heartache. But it is not for ever; because Jesus became a curse so that we can look forward to a world with "no more death or mourning or crying or pain" (Revelation 21 v 4).

Meditate

Hail the Heav'nly Prince of Peace!
Hail the Sun of Righteousness!
Light and life to all he brings,
Ris'n with healing in his wings.
Mild he lays his glory by,
Born that man no more may die,
Born to raise the sons of earth,
Born to give them second birth.

(From "Hark the herald angels sing" by Charles Wesley, 1707-1788)

∽

Prayer

Here I stand amazed and cry:
O the depths of the riches both of the wisdom and knowledge of God!
O wisdom, kind and merciful toward men in a wonderful degree!
Well may your loving kindness be called a depth of riches.
When you did commend your love toward us,
you would be so bountiful as to give your own self for us,
that we might be restored to you and to God.
Oh! Loving, gracious, beneficent wisdom!
You that were God's mouthpiece, Word and incarnate Truth!
Word, true in utterance, true in act!
You would teach us in human guise,
that we might gain the wisdom divine—
you would be in man,
that we might be in God.
You in your humanity would humble yourself to death,
even the death of the cross,
that we might be exalted to life,
even the life of God! Amen.
(John Colet, Renaissance theologian, 1467-1519)

Born to be exalted by the Father

"Therefore God exalted him to the highest place..."
Philippians 2 v 9

So far in this hymn in Philippians 2 the trajectory has been all downwards. Christ Jesus started off sharing the nature of God and enjoying equality with God. He never stopped being divine, but he did choose to step down from heaven. He laid aside the advantages of divine glory.

It was a big deal for the Lord of all the universe to become a servant. Though he was superior to the angels, he chose to share their status as servants of God. But Jesus went lower. He became the baby in the manger of Bethlehem. He shared our weaknesses, frailty, struggles and pain.

And then Jesus went lower still. He died—and he died a shameful, cursed death on the cross. He died condemned by humanity, betrayed by his friends and cursed by his Father. Down, down, down, until there was nowhere lower he could go.

- ๑ Step 1: He became a servant.

- ๑ Step 2: He became human.

- ๑ Step 3: He became obedient to death.

- ๑ Step 4: He became obedient to death on a cross.

But the story that begins at Christmas—and which is celebrated in this hymn—is "V-shaped". Christ went down until he reached the low point of the V, and then the trajectory of his story radically changed direction. From then on it was up, up, up. "God exalted him to the highest place" (v 9).

- ๑ Step 1: He was raised from the dead.

- ๑ Step 2: He ascended into heaven.

- ๑ Step 3: He is given the name above every name.

- ๑ Step 4: He will return to be acknowledged as Lord of all.

Jesus took what we deserved—the penalty of our sin. And then he received what he deserved—exaltation by the Father.

Where does Jesus end up? In the highest place. Higher even than where he started.

Today we still talk about a monarch "ascending" to the throne. Height continues to be a powerful image of status. Jesus is exalted and high because he is the King of the universe.

∽

Over 500 years before the first Christmas, the prophet Daniel saw a vision of four beasts, symbolising four great empires. Then God, the Ancient of Days, takes his place on the judgment throne and a court is convened. The beast-empires are destroyed. Then Daniel says, "In my vision at night I looked, and there before me was one like a son of man, coming with the clouds of heaven" (Daniel 7 v 13). The son of man comes before the Ancient of Days and is given everlasting dominion over all nations.

Few prophetic visions influenced the early church more than this one. They recognised Jesus as the son of man. And, just as the son of man in Daniel's vision had come with the clouds, so Jesus had ascended into the clouds, 40 days after his resurrection. At least that's what it looked like from below. But Daniel's vision describes what took place on the other side of the clouds. Jesus came before the throne of his Father to be given all authority over the nations. That's why Paul uses the past tense in Philippians 2 v 9: "God *exalted* him". His exaltation has already taken place. His ascension was his enthronement.

The story that began in the manger of Bethlehem ends with Jesus standing in glory before the Ancient of Days.

∽

Perhaps the key word in verse 9 is the word "therefore". The point is not simply that Jesus is exalted. The point is that Jesus is exalted *because* he was humiliated. He freely and willingly chose to humble himself for the sake his people. And because of this obedience to the Father's will and because of this love for his people, God has now honoured him. The exaltation of Jesus is the Father's response to the humiliation of Jesus.

Jesus ends up where he began: equal with God. But there is a difference; everyone has now seen the full extent of his love. Previously we fell before him in fear. Now we fall before him in love.

∽

Before he ascended into heaven, Jesus said to his disciples, "All authority in heaven and on earth has been given to me. Therefore go and make disciples of all nations" (Matthew 28 v 18-19). The ascension of Jesus is the basis for mission. We call on people to submit to Christ, because Christ has been given all authority. Our motivation for evangelism is not just that people need to be saved, but that Jesus deserves to be honoured.

Christmas is often a great opportunity for evangelism. Your church may be having a guest service or special children's events. Your neighbours may be open to a conversation about your faith, or an invitation into your home. And every time you speak of Christ, you are calling on the nations—your colleagues, your friends, your neighbours—to recognise that God has exalted him to the highest place. Your words may be faltering. Afterwards you'll probably wish that you'd put things differently. But don't be discouraged; you still speak with the authority of the One who has been given all authority. So keep on speaking about King Jesus.

Meditate

Let earth and heav'n combine,
Angels and men agree,
To praise in songs divine,
The incarnate Deity,
Our God contracted to a span,
Incomprehensibly made man.

He laid his glory by,
He wrapped him in our clay;
Unmarked by human eye,
The latent Godhead lay;
Infant of days he here became,
And bore the mild Immanuel's Name.

(From "Let earth and heaven combine" by Charles Wesley, 1707-1788)

∽

Prayer

Lord Almighty, the God of Israel,
enthroned between the cherubim,
you alone are God
over all the kingdoms of the earth.
You have made heaven and earth.
Give ear, Lord, and hear;
open your eyes, Lord, and see;
listen to all the words people have spoken
to ridicule you, the living God.
Now, Lord our God, deliver your people,
so that all the kingdoms of the earth
may know that you, Lord, are the only God. Amen.

(Adapted from Isaiah 37 v 16-20)

Born to spread his fame

"… and gave him the name that is above every name"
Philippians 2 v 9

There's a theory that people often end up doing a job that reflects their name. Obviously not always. Maybe not even often. But more often than average. John Baker sells bread. Tom Clark shuffles paper. Kate Taylor loves to sew. The fancy word for this phenomenon is "nominative determinism"—our names in some way determine who we are.

We see a version of this in the Bible. Often names in the Bible prove significant, especially when the act of naming is part of the story. Adam names his wife "Eve", which means "living", because "she would become the mother of all the living" (Genesis 3 v 20). Considering nominative determinism, perhaps it's no surprise that the next time Eve is mentioned by name she's having children.

Jesus renames one of his disciples "Peter", which means "rock", because Peter's confession of faith will be the foundation of the church (Matthew 16 v 18). Again, it's no surprise that Peter becomes the leader of the first church.

But in the Bible this link works in both directions. A person's name can also become the summary of their character. We still sometimes think like this today. When we talk of someone having "a good name", we mean they have a good character. Whenever people hear their name, they know that this is someone they can trust.

∿

What about the name "Christ Jesus" (as Paul calls him in Philippians 2 v 5)? The name "Christ" means "anointed one". In the Old Testament, the kings of Israel were anointed with oil—so the "anointed one" was the king. But as each of Israel's kings made a mess of their own lives and the life of the nation, God promised a coming Saviour-King: *the* anointed one, the Christ. Indeed, "Christ" was not so much a name as a job title.

"Jesus" is a proper name. It means "saviour". It wasn't chosen by Mary or Joseph. Joseph was told what to name the baby in Mary's womb by an angel: "You are to give him the name Jesus, because he will save his people from their sins" (Matthew 1 v 21). It's not quite nominative determinism. It's more that God is matching up the name of Jesus with his role. His name is chosen because of the role he's going to play in God's eternal plan.

∿

Now Paul says that God "gave him the name that is above every name". Jesus has so perfectly fulfilled the role assigned to him that he perfectly fits his name. There is every reason to call him "Christ", because he is fully and perfectly God's Saviour-King. And there is every reason to call him "Jesus", because he has fully and perfectly saved his people. And, because his name represents him and his character, it deserves to be honoured above every name. Whenever we hear the name of Christ Jesus, we know that this is a person we can trust. We know that this is someone who is above everyone else.

∿

The name of Jesus is beautiful, for his name encapsulates his character and work. Indeed, Jesus has many names, because one name is not enough to reflect all that he is and all that he has done. He is the Word of God, the Alpha and Omega, the Altogether Lovely One, the Lion of Judah, the Morning Star, the Desire of Nations, the True Vine, the Beloved of God, the Mighty God, the Resurrection and the Life, the Good Shepherd, the Prince of Peace, the Lamb of God, the Redeemer, the Bridegroom, the Light of the World, the Bread of Life, the Friend of Sinners, our Great High Priest, the Only Begotten Son. And many, many more besides. His work is too rich and too varied to be confined to one name.

All these names are precious to Christians. They are precious because each one in some way captures an aspect of who Jesus is or what he's done for us.

And it is not just Christians who find the name of Christ precious. It is, after all, God the Father who has given him the name that is above every name. The name of Jesus—the reputation of Jesus—is precious to God the Father.

∿

Look back over the list of the names of Jesus above. Think about the challenges you face this Christmastime. Is there a name of Jesus that speaks to your situation? Is there a name that is especially precious to you at this moment?

Meditate

How sweet the name of Jesus sounds
In a believer's ear!
It soothes his sorrows, heals his wounds,
And drives away his fear.

It makes the wounded spirit whole,
And calms the troubled breast;
'Tis manna to the hungry soul,
And to the weary, rest.

Dear Name, the Rock on which I build,
My Shield and Hiding Place,
My never failing treasury, filled
With boundless stores of grace!

(From "How sweet the name of Jesus sounds" by John Newton, 1725-1807)

∽

Prayer

Our God, we pray
that you may make us worthy of your calling,
and that by your power you may bring to fruition
our every desire for goodness and
our every deed prompted by faith.
We pray this so that the name of our Lord Jesus
may be glorified in us, and we in him,
according to your grace
and the grace of the Lord Jesus Christ.
Amen.

(Adapted from 2 Thessalonians 1 v 11-12)

Born to receive the praise of heaven

"… that at the name of Jesus every knee should bow, in heaven"

Philippians 2 v 10

When we imagine the coming of Jesus at the first Christmas, our feet are firmly on the ground. But what would it be like to look on his coming from the perspective of heaven?

"Glory to God in the highest heaven, and on earth peace to those on whom his favour rests" (Luke 2 v 14). Those are some of the most familiar words from the Christmas story. At a nativity play near you, they will be repeated by children wrapped up in sheets and wearing tinsel halos. An angel had just told the shepherds that a Saviour had been born in Bethlehem. And then "a great company of the heavenly host appeared" and filled the skies with their praise. This is how heaven greeted the birth of Christ.

The child in the manger went largely unnoticed on earth. A handful of shepherds witnessed his birth, but I imagine few people believed their crazy story. After all, shepherds were notoriously untrustworthy. Perhaps the residents of Bethlehem heard rumours of strange visitors from the east, but they came and went. But things soon calmed down and life went on.

But heaven had never seen anything like this: the Son of God taking on human flesh. The angels in the sky were only a glimpse of the glorious scene in heaven as the Saviour was born.

But the birth of Jesus was only the beginning. As Paul unfolds Christ's story in Philippians 2, Jesus steps lower and lower. Throughout eternity the Son of God had lit up heaven with his splendour. What, then, did the angels make of his humiliations, of his death, of the cross? "Even angels long to look into these things," says Peter (1 Peter 1 v 12). There was no heavenly host of angels appearing as Jesus died. No songs filled the skies. Even the angels lost their voices.

But all that changed with the resurrection and ascension of Jesus. God exalted him so that "at the name of Jesus every knee should bow", including the inhabitants of heaven. We can only guess at the euphoric reception Jesus received as he passed through the clouds at his ascension to appear before the Ancient of Days.

~

We do, however, have some clues from the book of Revelation. John is shown "a door standing open in heaven", and if we peer through carefully, we get a glimpse of heaven's perspective on the coming of Jesus. John sees God's purposes for history represented by a sealed scroll. But no one can open the scroll and unfold God's plan until the Lion of Judah appears. But what John sees is not a lion, but a Lamb. This is Jesus, the Glory of Heaven, having completed his work on the cross.

And it's at this point we hear the response of heaven to the story of Jesus—to the One who did not grasp the advantages of deity, but became a servant, became human, and died on the cross. First the four living creatures and the twenty-four elders say:

> *You are worthy to take the scroll*
> > *and to open its seals,*
> *because you were slain,*
> > *and with your blood you purchased for God*
> > *persons from every tribe and language and people and nation.*
> *You have made them to be a kingdom and priests to serve our God,*
> > *and they will reign on the earth.* (Revelation 5 v 9-10)

And then "thousands upon thousands" of angels join in:

> *Worthy is the Lamb, who was slain.* (Revelation 5 v 12)

∽

Christmas is an invitation to *sing with the angels*. The writer of Hebrews says that whenever you gather as God's people, "you have come to … the heavenly Jerusalem. You have come to thousands upon thousands of angels in joyful assembly" (Hebrews 12 v 22). When you sing your Christmas hymns, there are angels singing with you. The guitarist may be out of tune; the organist may be turning every carol into a dirge; your children may be fighting at your feet. But you are singing with the angels. And together we sing:

> *Glory to God in the highest heaven,*
> > *and on earth peace to those on whom his favour rests.*

> *Worthy is the Lamb, who was slain,*
> > *to receive power and wealth and wisdom and strength*
> > *and honour and glory and praise!*
> > > (Luke 2 v 14; Revelation 5 v 12)

Meditate

Sing, choirs of angels, sing in exultation,
Sing, all ye citizens of heaven above!
Glory to God, glory in the highest:
O come, let us adore Him,
Christ the Lord.
(From "Adeste, fideles")

∽

Prayer

Lord Jesus, our souls would track the shining way
by which thou hast ascended through the gate of pearl
up to thy Father's throne.
We seem to see thee sitting there, man, yet God,
reigning over all things for thy people.
And our ears almost catch the accents of the everlasting song:
"Worthy is the Lamb that was slain
to receive honour, and power, and glory,
and dominion, and might for ever and ever."
Lord, we say, "Amen".
From the outskirts of the crowd that surround thy throne
we lift up our feeble voices in earnest "Amens".
Though far off by space, we know that we are very near to thy heart.
Thou lookest over the heads of the angelic squadrons to behold us,
and thou dost hear the praises—yes, and the groans of thy well-beloved bride.
For are not we most near thee, thy flesh and thy bones?
We know we are. We feel the ties of kinship within us.
We our best Beloved's are, and he is ours ...
to whom be glory, world without end. Hallelujah!
(Charles Haddon Spurgeon, Baptist preacher, 1834-1892)

Born to receive the praise of earth

"... that at the name of Jesus every knee should bow ...
on earth"
Philippians 2 v 10

A t *the name of Jesus every knee should bow ... on earth.* Paul
doesn't mean "should" in the sense of "ought to"—he means
"should" in the sense of "will". And there are many times when
this line can seem like a joke. When was the last time your boss
or your neighbour or your prime minister or president bowed the
knee to Jesus?

Consider the conversations in your workplace. Evaluate the
decisions made at your team meetings or handed down by your
managers. Or the things taught at your child's school. Do they
reflect people bowing the knee to Jesus?

Consider your nation's media output. Evaluate the decisions
made by your government. Reflect on the norms of your culture.
Do they reflect people bowing the knee to Jesus?

Sometimes the answer is yes. You may live next door to a believer or work for a Christian organisation. Christians don't always get it right, but we at least try to live with Jesus as our King.

But for the most part, the people of earth do not bow the knee to Jesus. Humanity's rebellion continues. While heaven sings its praise of Jesus, earth mocks his name and ignores his will. It may well be that one or two examples from the past few days immediately spring to mind.

~∂

Yet, says Paul, God has exalted Jesus so that at the name of Jesus every knee should bow *on earth*.

Jesus was born at Christmas and humbled himself to death so that he might receive the praise of earth. And God is intent on seeing this happen.

Humanity's rebellion does indeed continue, but the story isn't over. One day Jesus will return to this earth. And on that day every knee will bow. Some will bow willingly, filled with joy as they gaze on their Saviour. Others will be forced to bow, filled with fear as they see their Judge. But, one way or another, *every* knee will bow.

~∂

So what's with the delay? Why does God allow the kingship of Jesus to be scorned so openly and for so long? The answer is *patience*. "The Lord is not slow in keeping his promise, as some understand slowness," says 2 Peter 3 v 9. "Instead he is patient with you, not wanting anyone to perish, but everyone to come to repentance."

The apparent credibility gap between Paul's hymn and our reality exists because God in his patience is giving people the opportunity to repent. God is giving people the opportunity to bow the knee willingly to a Saviour, rather than bow unwillingly to a Judge.

And this is where *you* step in. God has given us the task of issuing that summons and making that invitation. The angels were the heralds of Christ's first coming; now *we* are the heralds of his second coming. We announce the kingship of Christ—realised in heaven and coming to this earth. And we call on people to bow the knee. Of course, we are to do this with gentleness and respect (1 Peter 3 v 15). But nevertheless, we do it as ambassadors of the King in the name of the King. Indeed, this is precisely how Christ's reign on earth is currently exercised—through the mission of his people.

This is what the angel told Mary about Jesus:

> *He will be great and will be called the Son of the Most High.*
> *The Lord God will give him the throne of his father David, and*
> *he will reign over Jacob's descendants for ever; his kingdom will*
> *never end.* (Luke 1 v 32-33)

And this is what we tell the world: *Jesus has come and he is coming. He will be great and his kingdom will never end.*

∽

This is also what we pray. For Jesus taught us to pray:

> *Your kingdom come, your will be done,*
> *on earth as it is in heaven.* (Matthew 6 v 10)

This is a prayer for Christ to return: to come to reign on earth as he reigns in heaven. But it is also a prayer that we might anticipate that reign now as we bow the knee and proclaim Christ as King.

So today as you pray, get specific. In what particular ways do you need help to submit to Christ's kingship? In what ways will you ask God to use you to proclaim Christ's kingship?

Meditate

Joy to the world, the Lord is come;
Let earth receive her King.
Let ev'ry heart prepare him room,
And heav'n and nature sing.

Joy to the world, the Saviour reigns;
Let men their songs employ,
While fields and floods, rocks, hills and plains
Repeat the sounding joy.

He rules the world with truth and grace,
And makes the nations prove
The glorious of his righteousness
And wonders of his love.
(From "Joy to the world" by Isaac Watts, 1674-1748)

~

Prayer

Your kingdom come,
your will be done,
on earth as it is in heaven.
(Matthew 6 v 10)

Born to conquer evil

*"That at the name of Jesus every knee should bow ...
under the earth"*
Philippians 2 v 10

It's amazing to think that Philippians 2 may have been an early Christian hymn. Imagine those little congregations in the first-century Roman empire—often threatened by the state and scorned by their neighbours—singing these words together. What was the tune like? We don't know. But we do know that their praise was full of Jesus.

Philippians 2 may not be the only early Christian hymn Paul quotes in his letters. Colossians 1 v 15-20 is another possibility, and it's another passage that is all about Jesus. It begins:

The Son is the image of the invisible God,
the firstborn over all creation.
For in him all things were created:
things in heaven and on earth, visible and invisible,
whether thrones or powers or rulers or authorities;

all things have been created through him and for him.

(Colossians 1 v 15-16)

The visible things on earth were created in Christ. Waterfalls, mountains, palm trees, penguins. But so were the invisible things in heaven, the spiritual dimension. Angels, archangels, cherubim, seraphim, demons—all were created through him and for him.

But at some stage one of the angels, Satan, became filled with pride and led a rebellion against God (Isaiah 14 v 12-15). Angelic beings were created *for* Christ, but now Satan and his followers are *against* Christ. They were created to sing his glory, but now they spread lies about Christ. They were created to be his servants, but now they are rebels against his rule. They were created to fill heaven with praise, but now they are "under the earth".

∽

The good news is that the hymn of Colossians 1 concludes like this:

God was pleased to have all his fullness dwell in him,
and through him to reconcile to himself all things,
whether things on earth or things in heaven,
by making peace through his blood, shed on the cross.

(Colossians 1 v 19-20)

Christ reconciles *all* things, including both "things on earth" and "things in heaven". That doesn't mean Satan and his followers will be saved. What it means is that Christ has conquered Satan. Christ has undone Satan's work and disarmed him of his power. He has wrestled power back from Satan. Ultimately, it means that at the name of Jesus, even Satan shall bow the knee. There will not be any realm outside Christ's control.

So Christ rules over the spirit world as Creator and he rules over the spirit world as Redeemer. Christ was born into the world at Christmas in order to conquer evil.

∽

How did Christ conquer evil? Here's the surprise. One might expect Paul to say that it was through a work of power, or through the resurrection. But in fact Paul says that Christ conquered evil "through his blood, shed on the cross" (Colossians 1 v 20). Paul expands on this later in his letter to the Colossians:

> *When you were dead in your sins and in the uncircumcision of your flesh, God made you alive with Christ. He forgave us all our sins, having cancelled the charge of our legal indebtedness, which stood against us and condemned us; he has taken it away, nailing it to the cross. And having disarmed the powers and authorities, he made a public spectacle of them, triumphing over them by the cross.* (Colossians 2 v 13-15)

What was Satan's power over us? The Bible describes him as "the accuser" (Revelation 12 v 10). Satan accuses us of sin. Even now, he points out that we deserve condemnation. The evidence of sin, says Satan, suggests that we belong to him and not to God.

Imagine a loan shark who comes to collect money from you. For as long as you owe him money, he has a hold over you. But imagine a friend pays the debt you owe. "Paid in full" is written across the record of your account. The loan shark might still seem menacing when you see him around the neighbourhood. But he no longer has any hold on you.

This is what Jesus did at the cross. He took our "charge of legal indebtedness" and nailed it to the cross. He wrote "paid in full" across it with his own blood. And so Satan no longer has any hold on us. He has been disarmed. His accusations no longer carry any weight.

∾

But Satan has not gone away. Not yet. He still tries to make us feel guilty. But we're not guilty. Not any more. Our guilt has been nailed to the cross. And we can leave it there.

Is there a particular sin that fills you with guilt? Those accusations are the voice of Satan. Imagine that one sin written on a piece of paper and nailed to an empty cross. Imagine the words "Paid in full" written across the account of your debt. Imagine God saying, *I have made you alive in Christ and I have forgiven all your sins.*

Whose voice will you listen to today?

Satan still rages against God's people. But he has been stripped of his power. And when Christ returns, Satan will be defeated for ever, and we will never again hear the voice of the accuser. One day, even Satan will bow the knee to Jesus.

Meditate

God rest you merry, gentlemen,
Let nothing you dismay,
For Jesus Christ our Saviour
Was born upon this day,
To save us all from Satan's power
When we were gone astray:
O tidings of comfort and joy.
(Traditional English carol)

∾

Prayer

Grant, Almighty God,
that since thou hast at this time
deigned in thy mercy to gather us to thy Church,
and to enclose us within the boundaries of thy word,
by which thou preserves us
in the true and right worship of thy majesty,
o grant that we may continue contented in this obedience to thee:
and though Satan may, in many ways,
attempt to draw us here and there,
and we be also ourselves, by nature, inclined to evil,
o grant, that being confirmed in faith,
and united to thee by that sacred bond,
we may yet constantly abide under the guidance of thy word,
and thus cleave to Christ, thy only-begotten Son,
who has joined us for ever to himself,
that we may never by any means turn aside from thee,
but be, on the contrary, confirmed in the faith of his gospel,
until at length he will receive us all into his kingdom.
Amen.

(John Calvin, Reformation theologian, 1509-1564)

Born to glorify God the Father

"… and every tongue acknowledge that Jesus Christ is Lord, to the glory of God the Father."
Philippians 2 v 11

In heaven and on earth and under the earth. What's left? Nothing. "Every tongue [will] acknowledge that Jesus Christ is Lord."

The victory of Christ is growing and spreading in a way that's completely unstoppable. At his ascension he was acknowledged as Lord in heaven. And through the mission of the church his name is increasingly being acknowledged on earth.

In AD 33 no one in Europe acknowledged Jesus as Lord. And then, a few years later, Paul got diverted from mission in Asia Minor and ended up on European soil. And now, a few thousand years later, Christ is acknowledged as Lord by millions of people across the continent. In Paul's time the gospel was spreading out of Jerusalem to the north, south, east and west. And today it's continuing to spread to the ends of the earth. Across the world Jesus Christ is being named as Lord in more and more languages—or "tongues", as Paul puts it in Philippians 2 v 11.

One day Jesus Christ will return to reign on earth as he reigns in heaven. And every tongue will acknowledge that he is Lord.

∾

This Christ-hymn ends, "to the glory of God the Father". It's not just the hymn that ends in this way. The hymn tracks the story of redemption, which is the story of human history. And the goal of history is the glory of God.

> *Then the end will come, when [Christ] hands over the kingdom to God the Father after he has destroyed all dominion, authority and power. For he must reign until he has put all his enemies under his feet … When he has done this, then the Son himself will be made subject to him who put everything under him, so that God may be all in all.* (1 Corinthians 15 v 24-25, 28)

At the climax of history every tongue will acknowledge that Jesus Christ is Lord. Every eye will look upon his glory. And then the Son will point to the Father.

The point is not to play off one member of the Trinity against another. Quite the opposite. Father, Son and Spirit have been united in perfect joy and love. The Father's great delight is his Son, and the Son's great delight is his Father. The Spirit binds them together in this mutual joy. And, in their overflowing joy and grace, they created a world and redeemed a people so that we might share their joy. The Father longs for a people who will adore his Son. The Son longs for a people who will glorify his Father. The Father gave his Son to create a bride for his Son. The Son humbled himself to death on a cross to create children for his Father.

The Son's great aim is to create people who will worship his Father. All his humiliations have been driving towards this goal: "the glory of God the Father". This is the destination of history.

∾

I recently met a keen canoeist. I happened to mention that I fancied a go at canoeing along the river that runs through our town. He seized on the idea and was soon planning our trip. I didn't want to put him to any trouble. I feared I might be imposing on him. But it was clear that this was no imposition. There was nothing he enjoyed more than sharing his passion with people. If anything, he was looking forward to it more than me.

Jesus has a passion. His passion is his Father. And there is nothing he enjoys more than sharing that passion. He was born at Christmas and went to the cross so we could share the delight he has in his Father.

The story of salvation begins with the Father's love. Jesus didn't come to win God over or twist his arm into forgiving us. It was the Father's plan from the beginning, from eternity. And the story of salvation ends with the Father's glory.

∽

God's great purpose had become Paul's great purpose. The goal of his ministry, and of this letter to the Philippians, is that people might "hold firmly to the word of life" (v 16). "And then I will be able to boast on the day of Christ that I did not run or labour in vain" (v 16). To this end Paul is willing to be "poured out like a drink offering" (v 17). As Paul sees the Philippian Christians giving their lives in service to God, he says, "I am glad and rejoice with all of you. So you too should be glad and rejoice with me" (v 17-18).

"Be glad and rejoice." We swim with the current of history when we are glad to see people glorifying God. And we sing in harmony with the music of the universe when we rejoice together in God.

Christmas is a busy time. But make sure you create some time to share the joy of the Trinity. After all, this is what it was all for. This is why Jesus came: "to the glory of God the Father".

Meditate

Though an infant now we view him,
He shall fill his Father's throne,
Gather all the nations to him;
Every knee shall then bow down.
Come and worship
Christ the new-born King.

(From "Angels from the realms of glory" by James Montgomery, 1771-1854)

∽

Prayer

O God, who hast made man's mouth
and canst cause even the dumb to speak,
open our lips, we beseech thee,
that we may show forth thy praise.
Forgive us for our slow and stammering speech.
Cause the fires to burn in our hearts
until we can no longer hold our peace.
Grant that, through our humble testimony
to thy Son Jesus Christ,
our friends and neighbours may turn to him
as their Saviour and Lord, and magnify him with us,
in the fellowship of his Church,
for the greater glory of his name.
Amen.

(John Stott, Anglican minister, 1921-2011)

Born so we might shine like stars

"Then you will shine … like stars in the sky."
Philippians 2 v 15

I wonder if you've watched your child or grandchild take part in a nativity play this Christmas. Perhaps you can remember taking part in one yourself. What role did you play? A shepherd, perhaps? Or a wise man? Were you made to play the donkey?

Or perhaps you played the star?

The star has an important role in the nativity story. The Magi see a star and recognise (although we're not told how) that it's the sign of a king. Matthew 2 v 10 says, "When they saw the star, they were overjoyed". But it's not the star itself that fills them with joy. This is how Matthew puts it: "they saw the star" and then "they saw the child" (v 10-11). They were overjoyed to see the star because it led them to the child. But the child was the focus of their attention.

Indeed, the story of the Magi begins and ends with worship. "We saw his star when it rose and have come to *worship* him," they tell King Herod (v 2). And then, at last, "They saw the child with his mother Mary, and they bowed down and *worshipped* him" (v 11). Not worship of the star, but worship of the child.

And really that means the worship of a king. The Magi didn't travel all that way because they wanted to see a baby—there were plenty of babies back home. They travelled because they wanted to worship a king.

The star matters in the story because it lifts our eyes from the manger to see the throne. It forces us to look beyond the baby and to see the King. He's described as the "king of the Jews" in verse 2. But in the story he's worshipped by people from other nations. This King of the Jews is going to become the King of the world.

And that's how Matthew's Gospel ends. Jesus has died, risen, and is about to return to God the Father. And he says, "All authority in heaven and on earth has been given to me. Therefore go and make disciples of all nations" (Matthew 28 v 18-19).

The baby has become the King, and the King demands the worship of all nations.

∽

And now I want to offer you a role as a star—not in a nativity play, but in the drama of life. In the drama of life you can be a star. You can shine. You can light up the stage. For Paul says that it's possible for you to…

> … *become blameless and pure, "children of God without fault in a warped and crooked generation." Then you will shine among them like stars in the sky.* (Philippians 2 v 15)

This is your chance to shine! This is your chance to be a star.

So what do you need to do? It's very simple, though you may not like it:

*Do everything without grumbling or arguing, **so that** you may become blameless and pure … Then you will shine … like stars in the sky.* (Philippians 2 v 14-15)

What do you do? You "do everything without grumbling or arguing". Christmas Day may prove to be a great opportunity to put that into practice.

You're sweating away in the kitchen and *no one* is helping. You're sweating away in the kitchen and *everyone* is trying to help, but getting in the way. You've sweated away in the kitchen and then *someone* complains about the stuffing. No grumbling, no arguing.

Someone talks all the way through the *Doctor Who* Christmas special. Someone tells you to shut up just because *Doctor Who* is on. No grumbling, no arguing.

An old argument bubbles up again, or the family joke at your expense gets repeated. No grumbling, no arguing.

Your mum asks you to help when you want to play with your new present. Your mum asks you to help, but not your sister— which is "*so* unfair". Your brother steps on your board game or breaks your new present. No grumbling, no arguing.

Your friend fails to phone you, so you don't speak to anyone all day. No grumbling, no arguing.

This call to do everything without grumbling or arguing echoes the language Paul used right back in verses 3-4: "In humility value others above yourselves, not looking to your own interests but each of you to the interests of the others." We can shine like stars this Christmas if we do everything without grumbling or arguing, *and* if we put the interests of others first.

∽

What do you think your prospects are of pulling that off?! It's going to be tough. But, as we've seen, these exhortations are wrapped around a wonderful description of the Lord Jesus Christ. If you view yourself as a servant as Jesus did, if you choose to humble yourself, then your grumbles will soon dissipate. And if you view yourself as someone who is in Christ, on a trajectory that leads to glory, then your arguing will struggle to take off.

Humility is never easy. But this hymn tells us that at the resurrection, history was flipped on its head. All we think of as great and important will one day fade away. And what we thought was humble and unimportant will one day be exalted. And Jesus is the beginning of, and promise of, that coming great reversal.

The stories of the cradle and the cross put our grumbling and arguing radically into perspective.

Meditate

Brightest and best of the sons of the morning,
Dawn on our darkness and lend us thine aid;
Star of the east, the horizon adorning,
Guide where our infant Redeemer is laid.

(From "Brightest and best of the sons of the morning" by Reginald Heber, 1783-1826)

∽

Prayer

As with gladness men of old
Did the guiding star behold,
As with joy they hailed its light,
Leading onward, beaming bright,
So, most gracious God, may we
Evermore be led to thee.

(William Chatterton Dix, English hymnwriter, 1837-1898)

Born so we might share his glory

"Then you will shine ... like stars in the sky."
Philippians 2 v 15

A gold medal hung from the neck of the athlete on my television screen. "Is there anything you want to say to the public back home?" she was asked. "If you have a dream," she replied, "and you believe in yourself, then you, too, can be number one." It's one of the most powerful stories of our culture. Follow your dream, believe in yourself, work hard and you can make it to the top.

But a moment's reflection reveals how ridiculous this promise is. Only one person in that race ended up with a gold medal around their neck. Only one person can be number one. Only one person is elected president. Only a few make it to the top of their profession. Most of us can't be number one in our home or workplace, let alone on the world stage.

It's worse than that. So much of our grumbling and arguing arises because we're all competing for that top spot. We want to be first. Or we want to be proved right. We want everyone to acknowledge how good we are or what a good job we've done or how hard we've worked. We want to shine more brightly than the rest. But we can't all be number one. And so we career into one another, resulting in all the predictable collateral damage one would expect from an inter-personal collision.

In the end, there's only person who will be number one—and that's Jesus. In the end, *his* will be the name that is above every name. That's the message of this hymn. We will all bow the knee before Jesus.

But here's the twist: Jesus offers to share his glory with his people. Jesus is the one true Gift, and he's the Gift that keeps on giving.

∾

I once saw a burgundy Bentley parked in the centre of my city, with men in black suits standing stiffly in attendance and a crowd gathered around. From the chatter of the onlookers it became clear that the queen was in town, attending a service in the city cathedral.

Later that afternoon the Bentley drew up beside me as I walked home. The window slid down and the queen's head appeared. "Would you like a lift?" she asked. Moments later there I was, in my scruffy clothes, making polite conversation with Her Majesty on the backseat of her Bentley.

OK, so the second bit of the story never actually happened.

At least, not with the queen. But I've received an even greater honour: I have been invited to join Christ Jesus. Even though I'm hardly dressed for the occasion, I'm in Christ. And, as we've seen, being in Christ is like being in a car. We go where he goes. We're carried along with the sure hope of arriving at our destination. And our destination is glory.

∾

Have you heard of the hashtag "FirstWorldProblems"? A person complains, and then someone quips #FirstWorldProblems, or the complainant does it themselves in an ironic way:

- "Christmas dinner was ruined because the gravy was lumpy. #FirstWorldProblems."

- "It's a disaster—we've lost a piece of the new Star Wars Lego kit. #FirstWorldProblems."

- "I can't sync my new Apple watch. #FirstWorldProblems."

It's an invitation to view our problems in a bigger perspective. What do these things matter compared with war or drought or epidemics?

The version of the Christmas story told in Philippians 2 is an invitation to do just that: to view our problems in a bigger perspective—the perspective of the glory of Jesus, the glory he shares with us. And it's not just our problems. All our little loves and grand hopes and secret aspirations—all the things that fill our minds from day to day and year to year—are given a new perspective too.

And it is the Jesus celebrated in this hymn that makes all the difference. Yes, we're invited to shine like stars this Christmas. But the real star of the show is Jesus: the One who was equal with God, yet became a human baby; the One who was perfect in every way, yet willingly embraced our shame on the cross; the One who defeated death, sprang from the grave, and is reigning from heaven right now; the One before whom every knee will one day bow, to the glory of God the Father.

If we see ourselves as part of that big story, if we see ourselves *in Christ*, then we will shine like stars.

Meditate

He came down to earth from heaven,
Who is God and Lord of all,
And his shelter was a stable,
And his cradle was a stall.
With the poor, and mean, and lowly,
Lived on earth our Saviour holy.

Not in that poor lowly stable
With the oxen standing by,
We shall see him, but in heaven,
Set at God's right hand on high.
There his children gather round,
Bright like stars with glory crowned.
(From "Once in royal David's city" by
Cecil Frances Alexander, 1818-1895)

∽

Prayer

Set our hearts on fire with love for thee,
O Christ our God,
that in that flame we may love thee
with all our heart, with all our mind,
with all our soul, and with all our strength,
and our neighbours as ourselves;
so that, keeping thy commandments,
we may glorify thee,
the giver of all good gifts. Amen.
(An Eastern Orthodox prayer)

TAKE SOMETHING UP
FOR LENT

For hundreds of years Christians have observed Lent in order to prepare their hearts for Easter, so that they can fully experience the joy of God's glorious work of salvation.

Tim Chester's thought-provoking readings for Lent from the Gospel of John will help you to engage with the wonder of Easter and to marvel afresh at God's own Son dying on the cross for us.

BIBLICAL | RELEVANT | ACCESSIBLE

At The Good Book Company, we are dedicated to helping Christians and local churches grow. We believe that God's growth process always starts with hearing clearly what he has said to us through his timeless word—the Bible.

Ever since we opened our doors in 1991, we have been striving to produce resources that honour God in the way the Bible is used. We have grown to become an international provider of user-friendly resources to the Christian community, with believers of all backgrounds and denominations using our Bible studies, books, evangelistic resources, DVD-based courses and training events.

We want to equip ordinary Christians to live for Christ day by day, and churches to grow in their knowledge of God, their love for one another, and the effectiveness of their outreach.

Call us for a discussion of your needs or visit one of our local websites for more information on the resources and services we provide.

Your friends at The Good Book Company

UK & EUROPE
NORTH AMERICA
AUSTRALIA
NEW ZEALAND

thegoodbook.co.uk
thegoodbook.com
thegoodbook.com.au
thegoodbook.co.nz

0333 123 0880
866 244 2165
(02) 9564 3555
(+64) 3 343 2463

WWW.CHRISTIANITYEXPLORED.ORG
Our partner site is a great place for those exploring the Christian faith, with a clear explanation of the good news, powerful testimonies and answers to difficult questions.